The Waldensian Martyrs

Pam Vause

Bilby Books Publishing
www.bilbybooks.com

KEEPERS OF THE FLAME

The Waldenses stood apart and alone in the
Christian world; their place on the surface of
Europe was unique; their position in history was
not less unique; and the end appointed to them is
one which had been assigned to them alone.

Table of Contents

ACKNOWLEDGEMENTS

I was impressed to research and write about the Waldenses, who endured martyrdom for over five hundred years in defence of their faith and liberty.

To learn more about these people, my husband and I travelled to the Piedmont Valleys, near the French border, high in the Italian Alps.

We met Alder, who kindly took us to his forefathers' village and explained how they lived, raised their families, and cultivated their fields.

We also met Joanne and John, who shared their precious time escorting us to places of historical significance.

When we left these valleys, it was with mingled feelings of joy and sorrow. Joy because God had prepared the way and orchestrated the unlikely meetings with these people. The information given to us has enriched my story and given its structure. Sorrow, because we had to leave this wonderful place and its people.

I wish to thank those who spent time with us.

CHAPTER 1

Italy 1486–1488

Leaning against a large granite rock, grandfather was silent while Marco told his story.

'Nonno, all went well until I entered the village.' He stopped and looked up at his grandfather, who listened intently. 'The streets were deserted, shops tightly shuttered, market stalls empty; even the town's dogs were strangely quiet. I could only hear the lowing of cattle penned in the market bull-ring. The village was still, not a sound, not a movement. It was eerie and unnatural. He searched for words to describe how it felt. 'I then noticed, you know, the one who's slaughtering our people. He was leading the papal army,' he shuddered and took a deep breath.

'Si,' butted in grandfather, 'Albert Cataneo, Archdeacon of Cremona and supporter of Pope Innocent.'

'That's the one. He rode with his army across the bridge into Pinerolo, and they encountered no resistance.

When I turned the corner with my cart and produce, it was clear that an advance troop was already at work. Signors were prodded up the streets like cattle; hemp ropes dangled around their necks. Soldiers stripped and looted shops. Others were dragging timber or carrying straw to the market square.

A soldier came at me from the side street with a wine bottle in his hands. He grabbed my mule, and it jumped sideways, knocking the drunk to the ground. More drunken soldiers ran towards me, their hands grabbing at my reins. I

1

pulled the reins, urging my mule to trot quickly. We jerked forward and the soldiers dropped back.

As I passed the church a very different scene met me. A signorina was screaming. Nonno, I was terrified. There was so much terror in her cries that I felt sick. She ran from the church; kept stumbling and then fell into the street and lay there. Her gown was torn and there was blood on it.' Marco shuddered convulsively as he told his story. 'I watched a soldier come from the church. The soldier knotted his hands in her hair and pulled her to her feet. Then he took her back inside.' Marco drew a strangled breath that threatened to become a sob, but somehow, he held it back. 'I knew suddenly whatever befell that signorina was far worse than the drunks I had encountered further down the street.' He stopped, shuddered, and went on.

'Nonno, the wind shifted suddenly and there were billows of black smoke rising in the air. You know I could feel my heart pounding. I was so scared. I stood in my cart and shouted, violently shaking the reins, and turned the mule in another direction, and then I made him gallop out of the village.'

Nonno just nodded and sat sadly contemplating what Marco told him.

MARCO HEADED DOWN the mountain track passing birch and chestnut trees, carrying the lamb his grandfather gave him. He was tall and solid, and at thirteen years of age, he was considered almost a man. Entering open pastures, he could see his village Borgata Cyrus and his family cottage. The smoke from his mother's kitchen fire usually made him feel secure, but today it reminded him of the other fire. '*I still feel sick in the stomach when I think about the soldiers. I wish Pietro was with me, he would have known what to do. I wonder what Mamma would say if she knew,* he thought.

The ancient village Borgata Cyrus

Bleating from the lamb brought him back to his present situation. His father's voice could be heard as he led the family in prayer. Marco quietly opened the door and waited.

His mother was the first to look up. She stood and walked toward him. 'Marco we were so worried, what took you so long?' Looking at the lamb in his arms she sighed. 'Son, we sent you to help Nonno, not to bring home stray lambs. What happened?' Taking the lamb from his arms, she thought for a moment and spoke, 'I suppose it was caught in the highland thickets.'

Marco shook his head, 'No Mamma, Nonno gave it to you. He said to use it for the family.' He quickly looked at

Maria his six-year-old sister, who was whispering to their father and didn't hear. He flopped down on a bench near the table as tiredness washed over every limb.

Concerned, his mother's dark eyes watched warily. Her long black hair was always kept in a twist behind her head, but she now brushed a stray wisp of hair from her face and twisted her aching solid built body. She stood for a moment contemplating; nodded, then took the lamb outside to the courtyard and placed it in the barn's enclosure.

When she entered the room, she placed on the table a plate of freshly cooked pizza, covered in tomato sauce with fresh cheese. It smelled good. The familiarity and warmth of the room, with father by the fire, eyes closed listening to Maria recite portions from their handwritten Bible, now resting on mother's knees, brought back normality to Marco. He sighed, relaxed, quickly mumbled grace, and then thankfully ate.

THE NEXT MORNING Marco walked to the far pastures. He passed stone dwellings that were clustered together along the ridge. They had lemon trees and grapes vines hanging over their garden walls and vegetables could be seen between or behind the buildings.

Looking at the mountains, as he walked up the steep pass, he watched the early morning mist move amongst the craggy tips.

Marco climbed the mountain slope looking for their cow. He stood and listened to the cowbells. Each bell rang slightly differently, making a special melody, the melody of the Alps. *'There she is,* he thought. *I can recognize our bell anywhere as it has such a distinct tone.'*

4

Approaching their cow, he carefully placed hemp rope around her neck and spoke softly as he stroked her. 'Come on old girl, let's go home.' The cow walked quietly behind, chewing her cud.

When nearing home, Maria met him with her curly black hair protruding from under a woolly bonnet. She danced around the home yard, with red bare toes sticking out of old worn shoes. She waved her arms about, drawing the once long sleeves, higher in her outgrown dress. 'Look Marco, the lamb is following me. I am going to make it my special friend.' She started to sing. 'Maria has a special friend, a special friend.' She led the lamb with some rope. The lamb jumped and frolicked as she sang.

'Maria, you had better take it back to its enclosure. Mamma will be cross. You know she doesn't like us making friends with our farm animals.'

'But why Marco? I would love to have a little lamb as my special friend.'

'Just do it Maria, and do it quickly before Mamma catches you.'

He thought to himself, 'I dare not explain what the lamb's future is to Maria as she's too young, and I feel I'm too young for what happened at Pinerolo, but somehow I know that's not true, as I'm almost a man, and I have to take some responsibilities around here.'

Maria's high-pitched voice chanting to her lamb seemed to beat in time with the rhythm of milk squirting into Marco's bucket. He looked again as she disappeared into the animal enclosure.

Shaking his head he thought, '*It is said that children in the mountains are monsters with only one eye in the middle of their foreheads and they have four rows of black teeth. I dare say this is to keep people away from us. They haven't seen our Maria.'* Maria came out and stood with her hands on her hips, then turned and skipped inside. *'She's a healthy little signorina that doesn't stop prattling,'* he chuckled.

CHAPTER 2

BORGATA CYRUS

Ancient 1000 -year old chestnut tree

While working in the fields, Marco once again thought about that terrible day. *'I must tell papa. I don't know what he will say, as he taught me to be silent and careful, and I certainly wasn't any of those things.'*

Father watched Marco. He knew what happened in the village, and was very worried. They sat under the large ancient chestnut tree, eating their mother's bread with fresh soft cheese from their cow.

'Papa, it was a shock to be in the middle of an invasion

without you or Pietro and to see their hate and willingness to shed blood. It scared me.' An involuntary shudder came over Marco, as he recounted the horrific details. 'The soldiers had the appearance of devils. Their faces looked so evil and this is worrying me. How am I going to witness if I feel like this?' A small sob escaped Marco's lips and tears slid down his cheeks, which he quickly brushed away, hoping his father didn't notice. He rubbed his bare feet back and forth in the warm soft soil, trying to get comfort from the familiar softness. He stared down at his feet, not daring to look at his father as he fought to regain his composure.

Father patted his hand. Marco looked up. 'Marco you will go with another and he will be well experienced in the ways of the world, and don't forget help is only a prayer away.'

'Papa, why don't we stay in our mountains and not witness to the unbelievers in other provinces? Pietro said the Pope is angry because we contradict his teachings.'

'Marco, you saw how evil they were. We must share with those who will listen about Christ's love for them. They don't have Bibles and they're being tricked into believing all sorts of lies.' His father stood, stretched, and quickly continued. 'Son, I have seen many people grasp the truth of Jesus' love. It is a privilege to watch the light penetrate their darkened minds. It brings such happiness to all that participate in these studies.' He smiled, at the memory.

Marco thought as he watched his father. *'I never realized how kind and gentle papa's whiskered face is, not like those dark, thin drunken soldiers in the village.'*

Borgata Cyrus spring fed water

His father placed a large cane basket with vegetables and grain on Marco's back and then picked up his, and continued with the conversation. 'Son, we have been chosen by God to do this great work, and we count it a privilege, even if we must die.'

Thinking carefully about what his father said, Marco with the heavy basket walked slowly, with his head down, across the planted field with his father trudging close behind.

When at home after some discussion with mother, father called Marco, who had stopped for a drink at the well. 'Marco could you please go to Signora Duval's place and leave half the vegetables and all the grain with her, as her husband Antonio is too old to grow crops, and then go up to the higher summer pastures, where Nonno is staying in his Shepherd's hut. Give him the rest of the vegetables. Don't worry about the cow, as I will milk her.' As a second thought, he continued. 'It will be good when Nonno is back from the higher summer pastures; si, not so far to walk when visiting.' Walking over to Marco, he leaned closer and whispered into Marco's ear.

Marco's face lit up and he nodded. 'Si, Papa.'

He looked around for his little sister. '*There she is in the courtyard, licking wild strawberry jam off her fingers, and she's so busy that she hasn't seen me,*' he thought. '*Well, I will go before she does, or she will want to come.*' He quickly dragged the large heavy basket onto his back and headed up the mountain track.

Walking along the path, passing the other cottages with their home gardens and barking dogs, he came to the last. It stood with its front door dangerously close to the mountain's edge. Marco realized the mountain had slipped many years earlier. From the doorway, he could see down the deep gorge, with its naked crags, and cascading waterfall. Marco knocked on the door and wondered why their dog didn't bark.

'Marco comes in,' said Signora Duval. She then turned to her husband. 'Look how tall Marco is getting, Antonio.'

'Come, come,' said old Antonio with a huge smile, as he beckoned Marco to follow him.

When Marco stepped into the cottage, he could see through the window the long descending path that ran narrowly along the mountain's edge to the other valley.

Small noises turned his attention to the open fire, and there near the hearth was a large basket full of puppies. Their family dog fussed over each one of them, carefully licking and nuzzling their little bodies. Marco sat on the floor and picked them up, one by one.

'Which one would you like for your sister?' Antonio asked.

Marco looked carefully at each puppy. There were two females and one male.

'Well, that's easy,' he laughed. 'Mamma said I had to pick a male, so it will be this one. Look how big he is, and how striking his black and white markings are. He's a beauty, and Maria will love him. Grazie Antonio; can I pick him up after I deliver these vegetables to Nonno?

'Si Marco.'

'Oh! Where will I place your vegetables and grain Signora?'

'Place them on this table, and hurry back, I am sure Maria will be anxious to see her puppy.'

Marco slung the basket, now half empty on his back, and as he went out the front door, he replied smiling. 'She doesn't know about it. It's a surprise.'

Marco hurried up the narrow path. On the mountainside, tall trees with low-hanging branches barred his way. When he pushed through the branches, rain-sodden leaves brushed across his face. He stopped; he could hear sounds in front of him.

'Was it soldiers approaching the valley,' he thought. Gooseflesh rose down his back and his cheeks burned with shame. *'What would Pietro think of me? Well, I know, a baby that's what!'*

Ducking under the low-lying branches, he came onto the track. He looked up to see in front of him a horse and cart that stopped and pulled to one side for him to pass.

'Well, look who's coming to visit me. 'Are there problems at home son?' his grandfather asked.

'No Nonno, I am bringing you vegetables that papa and I picked this morning.

'Grazie Marco. If only your folk knew I was heading their way it would have saved you a trip. Well never mind, hop up and we can drive back together.'

'Nonno, I have to pick up a puppy for Maria, from the Duval's before I go home.'

'I must stop there as well, so we can do our errands together.'

Marco was in the cottage giving the little puppies the last cuddle when he heard his grandfather at the front door speaking to old Antonio.

'Do you think we could set up a watch, in your home for the next few months? I believe the army has been approaching the valleys and arresting folks. They have been dragging them down to the villages and,' he lowered his voice; Marco couldn't hear another word, but he knew what they were saying. With his heart now drumming louder than the soft droning of their voices, fear once again swept over him.

'Dear Lord, please take this fear from me,' he prayed. Quickly he gathered the male puppy in his arms and stepped out of the room.

'Are you ready?' said grandfather when he saw Marco walking towards them. He then turned and gave old Antonio a knowing look, as they still had many things to discuss, on the subject they had been talking about.

Grandfather placed on the porch table, chestnuts from his grove, meat from his herd, and several sheep skins tanned and ready for Anna to stitch together for their bed, as the coming winter would soon be on them.

'Grazie, Grazie,' Anna said, quickly kissing grandfather's right then left cheek. She turned and hugged Marco goodbye.

'NONNO, MARCO,' CALLED Maria as she ran out to meet them. 'I have a secret, a big, big secret and you must come inside and see,' she squealed jumping up and down, clapping her hands.

'Well, if it's a secret, you had better not tell,' Marco laughed, as he carefully stepped from the cart with his little surprise tucked into his jacket.

'Marco your jacket, it's wriggling about, what's in there?' Maria squealed pointing, now quiet and a little frightened.

'Come and see,' Marco laughed, squatting as he reached into his jacket, placing the little fluffy, squirming, bundle into Maria's arms.

'A puppy, is it for me?'

Marco nodded.

'Look what I have; a beautiful puppy, and just for me,' Maria shouted as she ran inside to the others.

Grandfather laughed, 'How quickly one forgets other surprises when there's a puppy involved.'

'And manners as well,' Marco laughed, as he walked towards the cottage's open door, while grandfather tied up the horse. Suddenly standing in the doorway was Pietro.

'Pietro, what are you doing here?' Marco laughed, as his

big brother lunged forward grabbing him in a huge hug, and holding him tightly.

'To surprise you all, that's what I am doing here,' Pietro said laughing, hugging, and partly lifting Marco through the doorway. 'How are you going little brother?'

CHAPTER 3

PINEROLO

Torre Pellice where the ancient women washed their clothes.

Marco,' father called. 'The summer is nearly over and we must sell our crops before winter sets in. This time I would like you to go to the Torino markets. Pietro, you must go with Marco as rumours are circulating through the mountain villages of more and more upheaval with the presence of the papal army.'

When Pietro and Marco rode through Torre Pellice their wagon rattled across a swift-flowing mountain stream. They turned to see women on the river bank, kneeling in wooden boxes with the fronts removed and the bottoms thickly covered in straw. In front of them were slabs of slate, on which they were slapping and squeezing their clothes. They used a stiff brush on the dirty spots. Pietro and Marco noticed others carrying wet washing on long poles back to their homes.

Later they travelled through flat terrain. The meadows were a carpet of colour, with red poppies and small white flowers amongst the summer grass. They rattled along and passed a small, barefooted boy leading slow-moving cattle with rhythmic clanging bells.

'Buongiorno,' Marco called and waved.

The boy waved.

Women with their heads down, dressed in dark coarse clothes, trudged beside their cart, carrying on their backs huge bundles of sticks for their fires. Others held poles across their shoulders, balancing large pots of water. Pietro noticed how their necks were swollen and deformed because of the poles.

Later in the day, they arrived at Pinerolo. The Waldensian Cathedral, a grand stone structure, stood on a mountain ridge looking down over the city and its fortified walls.

Some of the peasants, with their produce in carts or on their backs arrived at the city a couple of days early, to set up their stalls in readiness for the market.

Pietro called to a trader. 'Jacob, I will swap our fresh-grown produce for your home tatted lace and woven cloths. We will take them onto Torino as they will be greatly sought after by the passing traders travelling to distant markets.'

'Si, I accept your offer, as fresh products will sell well in this market,' the trader replied.

Leaving Pinerolo at daybreak, their mule pulled the small wagon filled with cloths, lace, and homemade farm tools, along the dusty track.

'MARCO, NOW THAT we're at Torino, we had better set up camp outside these city's walls. Let's do it quickly, as it looks like rain,' Pietro called, looking at the darkening sky with its threatening clouds. 'We can go into the market square tomorrow and set up our stall.'

The next morning, they noticed a crowd had already gathered on the city's edge.

'Pietro, look over there,' Marco pointed.

An air of excitement could be felt rippling through the crowd. They were waving banners and girls were reaching up to pass flowers to soldiers on horseback. Then the famous Lorenzo de Medici the 'Magnificent' rode by. He wasn't handsome as he had large dark eyes set close together and a long nose on small features, but his bearing was regal and his dress was grander than anything Marco had seen before. He was magnificent with his red silk cape glistering in the sun, and his cap covered in jewels. Even his horse was made brilliant with golden ornaments and silver bells. The people in dark drab peasant clothing cheered long and hard. Marco moved forward and stood amongst the village people. He was awe-struck by the pageant, but also fearful of the crowd. He looked for Pietro, who was talking earnestly to another trader with cart and produce. When Pietro saw Marco's pale anxious face, he shook hands with the trader and moved closer to Marco.

'Marco, let's go while we can. I was told that the market

is closed and today there will be drunk revelling in the city.'
He held out his hand to help Marco up onto the cart.

Once on the cart and heading out of Torino, Pietro
continued with the latest news. 'Marco, I will tell you what
folk are whispering about, but we mustn't speak of it here in
this place, as it will be very dangerous for all involved.' He
waited and didn't say anymore as people were still pressing
around their mule and cart, as they moved slowly through
the crowd, and out into the country.

Marco nodded, and fear once again clutched his
stomach. He sat quietly waiting for Pietro to start his story.
The cart bumped along the rough track, as people walked
past heading into town hoping to join the activities. Others
worked their vineyards, and their grand country villas could
be seen amongst the vines. Everything looked normal as
their cart rattled and splashed across a small creek.

*'What's so secret and so dangerous that it makes Pietro wait
until he is well into the mountains before he can tell it?'* Marco
thought as he looked at his brother's worried expression.

'Marco, the King of Naples's wife, owns the land on these
plains and near our valleys. The Pope has urged her to purify
the territory of heretics. That means our brethren, Marco.'

All Marco could do was nod.

'The Pope has drawn up a cordon for these districts, and
the Pope's bull is to be universal in its application. They
hoped to leave us ignorant of these facts and the commotion
it has excited amongst the local people. Thank God, the
cordon hasn't yet been placed over our mountain villages,
but we must get ready as they will try soon enough. We must
go home and warn our people.'

'Pietro what is a cordon?'

'It means it is an agreement with the duke and landowners for the Pope to place his soldiers around the borders of the villages on the plains. The soldiers will prevent people from entering or leaving these villages without their permission. We must warn the people before the soldiers arrive. When they take over the villages they will go from house to house and kill all dissenters of the state. They have been telling folk everywhere that 'wherever a Vaudois foot treads, the soil will be polluted and the air tainted' so the area is to be purified with Vaudois blood. The cordon has been drawn up to prevent our so-called heresies from spreading. They say this must be done for the health of the district.'

Reaching a village by midmorning they stopped to share the tales of future events that were rumoured to strike the brethren in the lowlands. They knelt together in great anguish and prayed with much pleading to their heavenly Father.

'It is the end of summer and much must be done I know, but we must think of our brethren in the lowlands and take time to warn them,' Pietro encouraged. 'Arrivèderci for now, and God be with you until we meet again,' he called as they drove away.

They continued with their mission, warning their brethren along the way. Thus, many days later they reached home, weary and saddened by the events, but not discouraged.

Mother and Maria rushed to the stables to meet them, while father very worried, stood looking over the villa's balcony.

On entering the kitchen, they could smell the familiar

odour of lamb with herbs and garlic, coming from mother's cooking pot, which simmered over embers in the open fire. Mother sent Maria to bed and then served father, Pietro, and Marco their meal, as they discussed together all the fearful news of the past few days.

'Our annual synod is due in a few months, but it will be too late,' mother worried. 'Papa you must contact all the different parish pastors and encourage them to meet immediately. We must quickly make provisions for these poor people, and organize matters to protect our mountain valleys.'

Pietro smiled tiredly at his distressed mother. 'Don't worry Mamma, the word has gone out, and in two weeks they will meet in our valley.

CHAPTER 4

SYNOD

*I*n the secluded valley with its circle of mountains looking down upon them, the churches of the Alps, the yearly synod was now in progress. One hundred and fifty ministers known as Barbs sat in a semicircle on the mountain slope. There were about the same number of laymen, with hundreds of youths sitting amongst them. They came from many different territories of the Alps. Further up the mountain slope, the women wrapped warmly in winter shawls and knitted bonnets, sat huddled together in small groups, watching the scene below. The children romped under the great oaks, on a carpet of brightly coloured autumn leaves.

Maria ran to her mother in her warm winter dress and boots, which Pietro had brought back from friends in the city. Cupping her mother's face in her hands she spoke. 'Mamma, will Marco be going away with the ministers.'

'No dear he's too young. He will go in three years when he's sixteen.'

'That's good, I don't want him to leave just yet,' she said and ran off to play.

Down the mountain slope, the men sat and discussed in unity, the terrifying future of their brethren in the lowlands; a future that was soon to be theirs. Each took turns to speak, none being higher than the other. A moderator was selected for the day.

Signor John de Vaux now spoke. 'In the past, we were nearly destroyed by the papal armies, which came into our valleys. In some areas, all were destroyed. We must do something to protect ourselves, or God's work will come to an end. God expects us to protect our families. First, we must give refuge to the seeking brethren from the lowlands, and if the army once again approaches, we must take up arms to protect our valleys.'

A murmur went up. 'Here, here,' and 'God is with us.' A vote was taken, and all agreed.

'Also, we must continue to prepare our youth, so they can win scholarships to attend Medical universities,' Father de Vaux explained. 'Our son Pietro's scholarship at the University of Firenze was organized by Doctor Solomon Michelini, our medical personnel. While at the University, Pietro had many contacts, with the ruling families of our Nation, and has sown many Bible truths.

Signor Jacques Caffarel stood and spoke. 'Also, our

winter boarding school of the Barbs in the valley of Angrogna must be supported. Young men from all the regions attend, and while there, they copy the Bible to share with others. They are also tested on their Bible knowledge and witnessing tactics, so they will be ready to go out with an ordained minister for three years. In this way, the Bible truths are scattered across the nations.'

One of the senior Barbs stood and announced, 'Could all the youth ready for dedication, please come forward.'

Twenty youths stepped forward and stood in front of the assembled Barbs. One by one they laid their hands upon the heads of these honest, young men. They could see for them not a rich benefit, but possibly martyrdom, and some 'God willing,' would come home at the end of their apprenticeship as ordained ministers to serve in their valleys.

At the day's end, the blended voices of the men could be heard in the sweet melody of a song. They sang:

> *God's Holy Words to impart,*
> *Across the world to yearning hearts,*
> *Ancient words given long ago*
> *Ancient words will guide us home.*

God's Spirit was felt and a renewal of their dedication to God was given.

PIETRO RODE ON THE narrow mountain pass, with the great oaks and silver birches, now almost bare. Wet, sodden leaves clung to his horse's hooves, making the ground slippery. He pulled his mother's thick, hand-woven cloak around his shoulders, against the chill, and thought of the annual Synod he had just attended. *'They spoke about soldiers in the past, attacking the valleys,'* he pondered. A feeling of fear crept over him, as he looked around wondering if soldiers were silently scouting the mountains.

TWO DAYS LATER, PIETRO reached the outskirts of Torino. Looking towards a country lane he saw something rumbling along a track that made his blood run cold. There were carts full of dead bodies, men following with spades, and scarves covering their noses. He looked across a small gorge and realized at the bottom, in a large pit, was the burial ground.

'I wonder what happened to those people. I don't think they were enemies of the state. They burn us,' he thought, with a shudder.

He rode through the open gates of the walled city. There weren't any soldiers guarding it. He hoped the people wouldn't recognize who he was. The gates lead into the older, poorer part of the city. The streets were narrow and had old rambling shacks joined together. There was hardly room for carriages. Pietro passed a butcher on the street. His clothes were grubby and covered in blood. He was cutting up a beast and threw the offal towards the drain, in the middle of the street.

'Hey, be careful you nearly hit my horse with your unwanted cuttings,' Pietro called. His horse danced about on the spot as black rats scampered unhindered about the poor animal's hooves.

The butcher looked up annoyed. 'Well, move on country boy. Who invited you?'

'Coming over!' called a woman from above. She leaned over and emptied a chamber pot out of her window.

Pietro ducked just in time. He looked around and noticed human excrement and animal dung on the street. The acrid smell of stale urine now offended his senses. The street was filthy and it stunk.

Pietro looked up at the lady in disgust. 'Don't you people clean your streets?'

'Just move on stranger. You sound like one of those dread Waldenses with their 'holier than thou attitude.' We have been told they rarely get sick in their mountain valleys. Demon possessed, that's what they are! If you are one of them you had better move on. We have permission from the Pope himself, to kill them if they come into our streets. Anyway,' she continued, 'didn't anybody tell you there's been another outbreak of the Black Plague?

Pietro was going to question her, as he knew through his medical training that the Black Plague was one hundred years ago, but before he could say any more, something up the street caught his attention. Men were coming out of houses dressed in black coats with white masks peeked in the front like beaks.

'*Black Birds,*' he thought. '*We were told all medical personnel must wear these garments when there is a plague. I must get out of here immediately. If it's the Black Plague all who breathe its contaminated air, die.*

CHAPTER 5

COUNTRY TAVERN

*P*ietro rode for several hours, until sunset. 'It's too dangerous for me to ride on my own in the dark.' He could see ahead, a small country Tavern. *'Perhaps I could trade some of Papa's furs for a room, and then start my journey early in the morning.'*

He tethered his horse in the stables. They were attached to the men's sleeping quarters by a thin wall with great holes that rats had gnawed. The women and children had a large dormitory near the kitchen; both buildings were separate from the main construction.

Passing the kitchen, he noticed chickens settling down for the night, on the roof rafters above the kitchen's open shelves, which held the inn's crockery.

In the pub itself, the Innkeeper a grubby man, who looked as if he had taken on the shape of one of the wine barrels, he frequently emptied, was struggling to move the family pig, which was determined to stay indoors.

'Get the creature,' shouted very dirty locals who cheered and laughed as they scratched their long-mattered hair.

'Catch him if you can,' one laughed.

'Keep it up, Artus. That's right, drag him out,' they laughed as they lent over their mugs of ale.

While Pietro was standing there, fleas jumped from the filthy food-scattered floor, onto his legs. He quickly hit the offenders off and moved out the doorway.

'This is how the plague spreads. I must get out of here and wash

as quickly as I can.'

He galloped his horse down the narrow farm track until he came across a small running brook. Riding his horse into the water he slid boots and all into its freezing current. He was careful not to wet his mother's cloak. Walking to the river edge he folded the cloak and placed it on a tree branch. When he removed his drenched boots, he thought of the Waldensian missionaries that returned home, in rags and bare feet.

'I wonder how they walked those filthy streets without shoes. I'm so glad my good friend Gerardo, gave me his old boots and plain school clothes, while we both attended University.'

He took off his outer garments and waded back into the water, and smiled at the thought of Gerardo's ornate clothing worn by him when not at school, while his horse Lilly kicked and splashed.

'Let me take off your load Lilly, and then you can properly roll,' he said quietly, and then removed the backpack. She rolled over into the cold running water. Pietro scrubbed himself hard with leaves from the nearby tree, and then Lilly's legs, as fleas had attacked her as well. She stood there snorting.

'Dear Lord, please don't let us get the plague.' The thought terrified him.

Before it was completely dark, he quickly gathered sticks and leaves for a fire. He was still in his wet clothing and shuddered with the cold. Soon the fire was blazing. Pietro now undressed and proceeded to rub on himself a mixture of vinegar and herbs.

'There is a saying that victims of the plague ate breakfast with their friends and dinner with their ancestors in paradise,' he mused

to himself.

When he was dry and dressed and had taken care of Lilly, he carefully retrieved his mother's cloak and laid it open on his knees. There inside, carefully stitched into the lining, were hidden waterproof leather pockets containing handwritten Bible text. They were written by his mother and Marco and in some places were whole Epistles of the New Testament. They had carefully hidden these treasures for him to share. He knew if the papal soldiers caught him with these Bible texts, he and all those he was witnessing would be killed. In the light of the fire, he read the written words he had been taught as a child. Lying down between his father's furs, he looked at the starry heavens and thought of Jacob, David, and other Bible characters who also slept under the stars, and then he drifted off to sleep.

Early the next morning he continued west through the lower flatter valleys of Lombardy for about another 10 miles.

'Si, I have been told about my ancient relatives the Albigenses, who once kept the pure early faith. In 1332 in the valleys of Lucerne and Peroca in France, they were set upon by the army, and many escaped into our Piedmont Mountains and valleys. It's happening again, here in the valleys of Lombardy. People are being killed by the Pope's army or by the plagues.

He paused and looked at the scruffy unkempt land where not even cattle or sheep grazed. As he looked across the plains it was the same as far as he could see. He alighted from his horse and reached for his skin flask. Gulping down the water, he kicked the dry dusty ground and thought about the past.

They say the valleys flourished with the Waldensian people working them. They were filled with rich fields, olive trees, and grapevines. Just look at them now, there's nothing. They also had opulent towns, and their homes were substantial. The people were cultured and their manners polished. The army set upon them, punishing them for their attachment to their religion. If we aren't careful the same thing will happen to us,' he reasoned to himself. *Lord, what will become of us?'*

As he continued with his journey, he thought about the family he was about to visit.

'If the Ricciardi's hadn't succumbed to the Pope, how did they survive? Si, the family survived, and they are still cultivating their original farm, and they still live in the original two-hundred-year-old villa. A very substantial place, I have been told.'

It was nearing nightfall. Pietro astride his horse ascended a steep track and came onto a ridge. He caught his breath, as he looked over the fertile countryside, with its rolling hills and open valleys that were covered in established grapevines, and olive orchards. The landscape was a patchwork of green and gold, with a scattering of tall pines, pointing their bony fingers into the sky, and the villas' red roof-tops glimmering in the setting sun.

After riding through what seemed miles of vines, he arrived at the entrance of 'Valli di Dio.' Turning into the villa's lane, he rode between tall pine trees flanking both sides. In front of him was a large well-established home. The square two-story stone building with its red-tiled roof faced the tree-lined entrance.

As he rode towards the front cobbled yard, an old man came from the side of the building and walked towards him. Pietro alighted from his horse and the man took the reins.

Pietro hesitated, *I don't know if I want him to take my horse just yet,'* he thought.

He looked around and noticed an elderly woman opening two large front doors.

'Are you Pietro de Vaux?'

'Si Signora.'

She moved forward. 'Welcome Pietro, I am Signora Ricciardi. I have been waiting for you.' She nodded to the elderly man.

'Leo will take your horse to the stables. Don't worry about your pack he will place it in your room after caring for your horse.' She stepped forward and kissed Pietro, on the right, and then the left cheek. The kisses were blown into the air in the casual Italian way of greeting.

She laughed at his surprised expression. 'Don't you remember me, Pietro? Your papa brought you here when you were a young boy.' She now playfully tapped both his cheeks with the palms of her hands.

'You have changed. You were such a strange-looking boy with long yellow hair and intense blue eyes. You were so tall and thin, and your long straight nose dominated your whole face,' she laughed. 'Now look at you; a strong young man, and quite a handsome one, I must say. I'm glad to see that your hair is much darker,' she said without tact. 'I would say it's now a chestnut colour. Wouldn't you?'

He looked at her greatly amused.

She wagged her finger at him and continued. 'You look just like your father when he was about your age. Si, he had mischievous eyes too.'

Laughing, Pietro took one of her hands and kissed the back of it. As he did so, he brushed against the many rings she wore. 'Signora Ricciardi, I am honoured to meet you,' he said respectfully, with a slight bow.

'Come, Pietro, you must be starving.'

Entering the two large doors, she led him through a wide cobbled passageway into a central courtyard. Pietro noticed on one side of the passageway a door was left ajar. Inside the room, there was a small Catholic chapel with candles, crosses, and paintings gracing its walls. Pietro was horrified.

'I was sent here to help Signora with the harvest. Surely Papa wouldn't send me to a Catholic home,' he thought. He looked at Signora Ricciardi, who understood Pietro's concerns.

'My forefathers after a lot of persecution gave in and became Catholics for peace and safety. I decided to go back to our original beliefs but I left the chapel as it was, to cover my real intentions,' she explained somberly. 'Let's go to the kitchen and get you something to eat.'

They walked through the courtyard with its running fountain spraying brown water into the air. Small bats swooped back and forth like swallows. On one side of the building there were stables, and on the opposite side of the courtyard was the winery. Large earthenware pots, filled with bright red flowers were dotted here and there. At the back was the kitchen, and next to the kitchen, were facility rooms. The servants' rooms were in this area as well.

They entered the kitchen and Pietro sat at a large wooden table while Signora Ricciardi fetched a servant. A young girl with eyes cast down entered and quietly served Pietro. He noticed her thick waist and heavy breast and concluded she was pregnant. Signora Ricciardi quietly watched. She nodded to the girl, and she left.

Signora Ricciardi spoke in a whisper. 'She was raped by papal soldiers five months ago. It is a very sad story, very sad.'

'Was it in Pinerolo when Cataneo passed through with his papal soldiers, and I believe many locals were burned at the stake?' Pietro whispered back.

'Si, that's right; her whole family was torched with the others in the village market piazza. She was saved, I suppose because they were busy having their way with her, in the church building. The soldiers had left her there to die. A local who was spared brought her to us.'

'My younger brother, Marco was there and witnessed all you have told me; she's a Waldensian.'

Signora Ricciardi looked surprised. 'Si that's right. How did you know?'

'Just by her demeanour, that's all.'

But Pietro thought to himself. *'It's that special Christian grace our girls have that makes them different, and even though she has been through so much I can see that it's still there.'*

'What's her name?' he asked.

'Judith Gonnet. Her baby is due in early summer. Come let me take you to your room. You must be exhausted.'

She quickly rose and led the way. Pietro followed her up the sweeping staircase with its open balconies looking down on the enclosed central court garden below. They passed the parlour, dining room, library, and a small music room, and there were several bedrooms. Pietro's was the middle room. 'Sleep well Pietro,' she said and left.

CHAPTER 6

VALLI DI DIO

Signora's Villa

A knock on the door woke Pietro. Signora Ricciardi stood in front of him in a multicoloured silk dress and cloak. It wasn't like the mountain women's attire. A large ornate gold clasp held her black hair in a thick bun behind her neck. Her finely chiselled features, black eyes, and long nose were more Spanish than Italian. She looked as if she was going to visit an important dignitary.

'Buongiorno Pietro; please meet us in twenty minutes in the central courtyard.' Signora turned and walked swiftly down the stairs.

Hearing voices at the front door Pietro looked over the balcony to see Signora Ricciardi greeting a young couple with a small baby. When he looked through the large heavy double doors, he saw a horse-drawn cart with more people approaching the villa. They were all dressed in their best simple farm clothes.

'I wonder what's going on. I must get dressed, as Signora requested, and meet 'us' as she said, whoever 'us' is,' he thought as he entered his room.

When he went downstairs into the courtyard, Signora introduced him to the small group. 'Pietro, my friends and I meet each Sabbath to worship here in my home. This has been my custom for many, many years. To worship openly would bring the wrath of the papacy on our heads. Only those I trust are welcome to participate in these services because the wrong person could bring death to all present.' She turned and asked about some other folk, and when she realized they couldn't make it, she continued talking.

'Well let's move into our secret worship chambers, the others will not be arriving today. Please follow me, Pietro,' she said over her shoulder as she entered the kitchen. She opened the door of a large larder and clicked something on the back wall of the pantry shelves that were lined with racks of wine from the property. The wall of clay bottles opened and stairs were revealed. Signora Ricciardi lit a lamp that sat on a nearby shelf and descended a strong well-constructed staircase. When at the bottom she turned, holding the lamp out in front so all could see the stairs.

'Please watch your step,' she said as they walked carefully down. While leading the way she lit small lamps positioned in recesses in the wall. Soon they all could see clearly as they walked through a narrow underground passage. Signora opened a door at the end of the passage and they were suddenly in a large storage room, which held the family's vintage wines. It was situated below the main winery that held a large wine press and wooden barrels with maturing wines. Candles had been lit in readiness for their arrival. The seats were large and comfortable, as in the villa's parlour, and were set informally.

When all were seated the service began. Signora used the family's large handwritten Bible and all listened to the wonderful truths read from it. Only a few people were privileged or interested in hearing these truths. Most people couldn't read and didn't own a Bible, and were happy to believe whatever the priest told them.

Pietro stole a look at Judith. She sat quietly listening to the Bible and her face radiated peace and joy.

'Thank you, Lord, for being with Judith and not letting that terrible ordeal rob her of her faith and trust in you,' he silently prayed.

The baby with the young couple started to cry, and the mother moved to a corner to nurse her. Suddenly old Leo appeared through a secret door behind the urns.

'Signora, unknown to me papal soldiers were snooping near the cellar and heard the child cry. You must get everyone to hide in the underground passageway, and take the young family into the above winery, as they know they are here.'

'Grazie Leo.'

She turned to the young couple. 'We are relatives, so they'll not worry you. Follow me into the above winery. Quickly now before they see us come through the hidden door.'

'The captain thumped on the front door of the villa. He was sure at long last he had caught Signora Ricciardi holding an illegal church service.

Leo hurried through the underground passage and arrived at the front door as the captain thumped upon it.

Pietro, unseen crept up the stairs into his room. He had to hide his belongings. If seen they would bring immediate trouble to all present in the household.

Leo stopped and caught his breath and then opened the front door. 'Can I help you, captain?'

'Let us in. We know what you're up to.' The captain pushed past Leo. Pointing to the stairs, he instructed ruffians that now represented his army as soldiers. 'Check all the above rooms and then down here. Bring the dissenters to me,' he yelled. 'We will show them what happens to trouble makers of the church.'

The soldiers ran through the rooms searching all the hidden corners. As they went, they stripped beds; upturned cupboards, and pulled out drawers, thus leaving havoc throughout the rooms.

When two soldiers came to Pietro's room, they found him sitting on his bed. He stood and in the most indignant voice he could muster, yelled. 'What do you think you're doing? Get out of my room and this house Do you hear me; get out now.' He walked towards the soldiers with a hand on his sword, ready to draw it from the sheath. The soldiers backed away, and when at the door, bolted quickly downstairs.

'Go to the winery at once. A baby was heard in that direction,' the captain yelled to no one in particular. 'No, I will go there myself,' he barked. 'You,' he snarled at Leo, 'will open the door and let us in to inspect the room, do you hear,' he snapped as he roughly shoved poor old Leo across the cobbled courtyard, to the internal door.

When they arrived at the door, Signora Ricciardi and the young family came out of the room.

'Can I help you, captain,' Signora said between clenched teeth.

'These people Signora, and the cart out the front?'

'Captain let me introduce you to my cousins. I have been showing them around the winery. We are going to have this lovely vintage wine for dinner. Look I will give you a flagon as well.' As she handed him the wine, she saw soldiers coming out of the above rooms, laden down with her possessions.

Going red she clenched her fist and yelled. 'Captain, I am a good friend of Duke Lorenzo Medici of Firenze and he will be passing this way with his cavalry. Place back my things immediately,' she shouted, waving her hands towards the pugnacious soldiers. 'I hope you haven't destroyed my home, and if so, your head will be on the chopping block.'

'Move out now. Move out now,' the captain yelled through the villa's open door, to his soldiers.

'Captain, I am reporting you. Do you hear me? We will have Duke Lorenzo's army waiting for you and your so-called soldiers, the next time you come anywhere near this property,' she yelled stamping her feet, and shaking her fist at the captain and his retreating soldiers.

The captain turned and addressed his men who were staggering out, laden down with valuable nick-knacks from the rooms. 'Stupid Becchini robbers take back Signora's jewels and all the other things you have stolen, or I will have your heads myself,' he bellowed.

'Stupid, stupid Becchini robbers,' Signora Ricciardi screamed, shaking her fist. On their way out she managed to give some a hard kick in the shins or a thump on the back. They snarled and clenched their fists, but didn't dare take action. Their lives were now on the line.

'Soldiers, let me check your clothing,' demanded the captain, as the thieves ran from the courtyard. 'If I find anything on you, I will kill you myself, right here on the spot.'

After a quick check, they mounted their horses and galloped away. Signora stood watching the army disappear down the lane, and slammed the heavy front doors behind her and she retreated to the kitchen to help those in the hidden passage.

THE NEXT DAY PIETRO, Judith, Jeanne the housemaid, and her husband old Leo picked up tools from the cellar and headed to the vineyards.

'Look, this is how you prune the vines. See, you must cut them back to the last bud. Do this with each branch, leaving only small twigs on the stumps,' Leo explained as he demonstrated by cutting off some of the branches.

The women took the clippers and proceeded to follow old Leo's instructions, while Pietro gathered and carted away the branches in a large wooden barrow. They worked for some time in the sun.

Pietro studied Judith intently, disturbed by the feelings stirring in him. She was very beautiful. Her Christian demeanour and gracious manner attracted him. He wondered if she realized how he felt. He turned from her, willing himself to concentrate on the job at hand.

After working for some time, Pietro stopped and stretched. It was hot and he needed a drink. His attention was drawn to Judith. Her blue eyes were dark with exhaustion, her cheeks smudged with dirt. She looked up at him, now her expression was full of appeal.

Old Leo also noticed her exhaustion. 'Judith we would like a meal, please go with Jeanne and help with its preparation.'

'Grazie,' she said in relief, saying a silent prayer of thanks, as she followed old Jeanne into the villa.

Pietro sought Signora; he had to talk with her about Judith.

He thought to himself. *'She is in no condition to work so long in the heat.'*

He found Signora in the front courtyard with two strangers. The older man spoke. 'It's enough that I have told you, 'He snapped and then drawled sarcastically. 'You said you would hide my friend if I told you.'

'What, right now?' she answered shocked.

'Si right now,' he snapped.

'I need to take refuge,' the younger signor said. Don't worry, it will only be until they pass by, which will be tomorrow.'

She cast a cursory glance over her shoulder and noticed Pietro walking toward them. 'Si, Si, I agree, just go now,' she said to the older man, waving her hands in the direction of the road. She walked him out of the courtyard, leaving the younger man standing there. He waited patiently, as he watched the birds hopping under the fountain's spray.

Pietro walked into the kitchen, giving Signora some

privacy. He wondered what the obnoxious man wanted. She had acted in a very vulnerable manner, which was so unlike her.

CHAPTER 7

DUKE LORENZO

The household had retired and didn't hear Signora Ricciardi talking to old Leo in the courtyard. With old Leo's help, she saddled two horses and rode with the young man to a neighbour's hamlet, many miles from 'Valli di Dio,' and returned late that evening.

The next day Pietro, old Leo, and his wife Jeanne worked silently together in the vineyard, intent on their hot activities. Pietro crouched down and picked up the last branch, placing it in the barrow. He then stood, stretched, and wiped his sweaty brow on his sleeve. He noticed heavy grey clouds had formed overhead, making the day unusually humid for early autumn. He turned to go but saw Judith walking towards them. She hugged a heavy water pitcher against her chest and right shoulder. It drew her loose dress close across her stomach. As Pietro watched, a feeling of tenderness came over him, for the girl and her predicament. She looked up, and their eyes met. She smiled shyly, and Pietro's heart skipped a beat, and he grinned foolishly.

Now standing in front of him she spoke in Patois; their highland tongue that originated from French mixed with Italian. She spoke with the soft native brogue. 'I have drawn cold water for you. Drink, you must be thirsty.'

Longing for home, a keen sense of kinship towards her came over him.

'Grazi,' he said, as he took the jug and drank thirstily, spilling water down his face. When he had quenched his thirst, he looked closely at her. Her hair was fairer than his as a boy, and her eyes lighter. She was tall and thin, with boney features; a pure Huguenot originally from France. Her light blue eyes stared intently back. His cheeks now burnt. Feeling unsure of himself, he quickly turned away. She understood, as she felt the same and was also struggling with her emotions.

He now concentrated on the sound of clippers snapping at the vines, and then another sound could be heard. It was horses, many horses. He looked up to see an army regiment on the distant road, fast approaching 'Valli di Dio.'

'Was the knowledge of this approaching party, the message delivered to Signora the night before,' he wondered.

Three men, Duke Lorenzo of Firenze, his General, and the regiment's priest now cantered down the laneway, leaving the regiment in formation on the road, outside 'Valli di Dio.' They were receiving orders from their Sergeant, who waited with them.

Old Leo indicated by nodding his head, for them to leave their pruning and go into the servant's quarters. They hurried away, except Pietro, who was curious about the unfolding events. With head down he slowly pushed his barrow, walking along the border of the vineyard that flanked the laneway. When the soldiers were level with him, he ducked down behind the barrow pretending he was picking up something from the ground, and in doing so, he missed seeing their faces. He quickly stood and went to the backyard to clean up, in case Signora called him.

SIGNORA STOOD AT the door waiting. She stepped forward and approached the horsemen. Duke Lorenzo the

Magnificent, stepped down from his horse and walked over, took her hand, and kissed it. They spoke for a while and then he quickly left.

Pietro missed all of this while he scrubbed under a fountain of fresh spring water, which ran into a trough, at the back of the villa. When he walked into the courtyard, Signora was talking to old Leo, by the stable door.

She looked up, and walked towards Pietro, as she spoke. 'Oh, Pietro there you are.' When next to him, she leaned forward and spoke in a low quiet voice. 'Duke Lorenzo and his General and priest will be staying here for two evenings and will dine with us tonight. The other soldiers will be camping by the river.' She noticed his shocked expression. 'Sorry, there wasn't a thing I could do. I told them my great-nephew on my sister's side was visiting. You must hide your things under your bed. We don't want them to know you are a Vaudois, as it will cause trouble and maybe death for my household. I have left my deceased husband's clothes on your bed. You must wear them while they are here, and please only use the dialect and customs of the elite in this area. I know you can because you have been boarding for four years with their sons at Firenze University.'

'Si, Signora,' Pietro replied somewhat cross because Signora was drawing him into a dangerous web through her association with these people, but she might need his help, so he went along with it.

When Pietro entered the drawing room Duke Lorenzo and Signora Ricciardi were sitting at the table in deep conversation. The other two men were leaning against the fireplace mantle, facing a large hearth, which held a glowing fire. Pietro hesitated in the doorway.

43

Signora noticed him. 'Pietro please come in and meet my guest.'

The other two men swung around. Pietro caught his breath. He recognized one.

'Duke Lorenzo, I wish to introduce my nephew Pietro de Vaux,'

Pietro stepped forward and shook the duke's hand with a slight bow.

Standing at the fireplace was a priest in black robes with a thin pointy nose and lank hair. He watched with an alert dangerous look, like a black cat that could smell a nest of baby rats.

'Father Francis, I would like you to meet my nephew Pietro de Vaux.'

Pietro shook hands.

'De Vaux, I have heard that name. Isn't it the name of a clan in the mountains,' the priest asked Duke Lorenzo.

The other young man at the fireplace now spoke. 'Father Francis, I wish to differ from you, this is my friend from college. Do you know any mountain folk smart enough to become doctors like my friend standing in front of you at this very moment?' he responded with a smile. Laughing he grabbed Pietro's hand. 'We meet once again dear friend.'

'Gerardo Usumari,' Pietro laughed. 'I've wondered what happened to you since we finished studying. It's been over a year now.'

Gerardo grinned and nodded and spoke of his current employment.

'So, you have joined your uncle's regiment and become his General. Good for you,' Pietro lied.

'I have heard everything about you Pietro,' joined in

Duke Lorenzo. 'We need somebody to manage the 'Mercy of Firenze Hospital. A talented and sound-minded surgeon like you is exactly what we need, especially amongst the poor in our ghettoes, as the Black Plague is breaking out in these places once again. Our people are afraid they will become infected, so the city needs an educated health worker. What do you think?' he asked.

'Grazie,' Duke Lorenzo, may I have a day or two to think about your most kind offer.'

All looked around at the priest, who was watching slyly with a cunning look on his countenance. 'Don't forget Sunday morning. All in this room will be going to the local village Chapel for Mass,' he said with a sneer.

Pietro didn't dare answer or look in the direction of Signora. At that moment Leo and Jeanne entered with their meal. While they were sitting with the guests and eating their meal the conversation continued between Duke Lorenzo and Signora.

'I have business and meetings to attend in this district. Will it be alright for my regiment to rest by the river while we are away for the next few days?

'Si,' Signora nodded.

'We will be back late Saturday evening so don't wait up for us, but Sunday morning we will accompany you to the Chapel,' the duke smiled.

The next morning, when the visitors left, Pietro met Signora in the kitchen for breakfast.

'Signora what will happen when your guests arrive, on Saturday for church? The soldiers are still at the creek which is near the entrance of the property.' After some thought, he continued, 'I will go through the field further down the lane and warn them.'

'It's alright Pietro, I warned them the other night, when I took the stranger to our neighbours.'

'How did you get caught up in this mess Signora? Why are they making us go to the Catholic Church?'

'They are testing us, Pietro. We have been in this bind for many generations now.

My kinsfolk shielded themselves from death by obtaining from the local priest a testimonial certificate declaring them to be Catholic. He promised they could keep the Sabbath in their homes if they did this. To obtain this certificate they had to attend the Catholic chapel, go to Mass, confess their sins, and have their children baptised by the priests. These days I only go when they ask me which isn't often. They know I have my Catholic chapel here on the property. The families who sent their children along for baptism and confession eventually became Catholic. Our old faith in most cases has died.'

PIETRO SAT THINKING while accompanying Signora in her carriage. *'How easy it is to run before the Lord. I also seem to be ducking for cover. Perhaps if I trusted God more and myself less, I would be more like my kinsfolk in our mountains. Si they wouldn't put themselves in compromising positions in the first place. Being away from home for so long, the world doesn't seem so wicked. Please make me Lord, more aware of the danger and not be so impulsive.'*

Signora's carriage's un-sprung wheels rattled and bumped along the stony dirt track, while Lorenzo and his men cantered in front. As the carriage approached the village chapel, people crowded into the small laneway, calling and waving.

The people crowded into the chapel's portico. As the party entered, they stepped aside for Duke Lorenzo and his men but folded in around Pietro and Signora like a heavy blanket thus restraining them from moving forward. Quickly Pietro and Signora were separated from the others, and the crowd squeezed and jostled them to the side, pushing them into seats towards the back.

With incense rising, and the priest's voice chanting, Pietro kneeling next to Signora heard her mumbling to herself, or was it to God? 'Caves of robbers may God confound thee. Caves of robbers may God confound thee. Caves of robbers may God confound thee,' over and over she muttered her chant.

'I wonder if she feels this makes it right with God,' Pietro thought.

CHAPTER 8

BECCHINS

*G*rey clouds hung low in the sky and rain threatened. Pietro drew his mother's cloak closer and nudged his horse into a gallop. While attending the nearby village he met as arranged, his friend from Bobbio Pellice. His father would receive his message and come quickly.

Crossing the creek, he noticed that the army had dispersed. *'They would have left soon after daybreak. I will meet my friend Gerardo and Duke Lorenzo at the 'Mercy of Firenze Hospital' in four weeks, but in the meanwhile, I have to wait for Papa. I am thankful that I'm not travelling back with them as in the evenings the soldiers will be drunk and revelling,'* he thought.

As he descended the hillside beside 'Valli di Dio' he could see old Leo and Jeanne in the orchard behind the villa, picking the last of the season's olives. He was anxious to return as he had something very important to tell Judith.

Entering the driveway, he noticed at the villa's door, Signora Ricciardi talking to a scruffy black-gowned priest, accompanied by a group of very strange-looking men. He rode up to them and tethered his horse to a post near the fence.

'I have never seen such a party before. I must approach them in case Signora needs my help. What is he carrying under his arms? It looks like a very large black book,' he thought.

The priest and the group of ruffians noticed Signora Ricciardi's face and all turned to see a young man approaching them.

'Pietro, these men are taking the yearly census for this area, but Pietro it doesn't concern you, so please go in and have something to eat,' she begged in a warning tone.

He realized what he had walked into. His father had spoken of it, and he knew suddenly the danger he was in.

'Grazie Signora,' he said.

Walking to his horse, he untied it and started to move away. They all watched.

The priest yelled. 'Not so fast Signor. When we visit, we have to record the names of all staying here on this estate. Also, we must know their heritage. By the look of you and the clothes you are wearing, you are a cursed Waldense.'

With this, he shook his fist at Pietro and the ruffians immediately set upon him, holding him down with their filthy hands. He realized immediately by their stench and strange looks who they were.

'They are 'Becchini dwarfs; brutalized, deformed street urchins, that murder, and of late force their way into the houses of people dying of the plague, and drag them, still alive, away to join the ranks of the dead, unless the signors give over money for their safety,' he thought.

He looked at their deformed features, evil eyes, and the rough goat hides, that they wore for warmth over their rags, and wondered why the papacy was using such people. He answered in his mind his thoughts. *'Because the Pope's army is always at war and its soldiers are being killed, and the genuine priests helping others, are dwindling in numbers that's why.'*

The large birch switches, which they carried, were now raised and were about to be brought down on Pietro's back when Signora yelled. 'Don't you dare touch him, do you hear,' she screamed. 'He is my nephew and is not from here.

He works for Duke Lorenzo as a surgeon at the 'Mercy of Firenze Hospital.' The duke's province isn't under your jurisdiction!' she added.

'That may be so, but we have to record all his details because he's residing with you at the moment and he looks to me to be a Waldense, and worse than that he looks like one of those cursed mountain Vaudois men. I believe they must be exterminated at all cost.'

'Well, what he looks like to you isn't important, and who said he is residing here? This is only your opinion.'

At this, Pietro flung the many filthy vagabonds off his arms and moved quickly to the back of the villa to its water faucet. At all costs, he must scrub himself, in the hope of removing any possible diseases.

'Well Signora Ricciardi, by law you have to let me in so I can write up my ledger.'

'You can come in, but not those disease-ridden Becchins' you drag along.' She slammed the heavy door behind her and the priest, leaving the vagabonds outside.

The priest stood in awe as he looked around the courtyard, with its large pots of coloured flowers, its running fountain, also the sweeping staircase and balcony with its ornate balustrade. She led him into the chapel and pointed to a small table at the door for him to place his book. She went upstairs to her room and retrieved her box with ledger books on farm business. While she was away, he busily scratched with his quill and ink that he brought in a small container, recording the encounter with Pietro, noting especially this man had all the characteristics of a cursed Vaudois.

PIETRO SAT IN THE warm kitchen with his head down sadly contemplating the past events, while Judith kneaded fresh soft dough into loaves on the kitchen table.

'Judith I always seem to be in the wrong place at the wrong time, but I'm concerned for others. We were taught to be silent and resilient and watchful in what we say, but as a medic, I am mixing with many people from all walks of life. At times, I feel I am denying my Lord,' he sighed.

'Pietro, I think you are afraid and I understand this, but you must rely on God more and yourself less. When you were in the mountains you stood firm, but now, because of your position as a 'doctor of medicine,' you want to be all things to all people. Pietro, remember who you are and be more watchful and less trusting of your friends. You should have been firmer with Signora. Having dinner with Signora and your friend Gerardo, you've put yourself in great danger. Please Pietro don't compromise your faith. By mixing with unbelievers, bit by bit you will lose more and more of your Waldensian heritage. Signora has been very kind, but she isn't one of us, and she is certainly not one of them. Through having her feet in both camps for so long, with all her compromising she has lost her spiritual zeal. Soon she will lose Jesus altogether and won't even realize it.' Judith placed her loaves in the wood oven.

'Si, you are right, I must be more watchful. By the way, are you happy that Papa will be taking you back home to our village?

'Si, Grazie, she smiled. 'It will be safe there.'

Signora walked into the kitchen with a big book under her arm and an even bigger grin. 'They have gone, and look what I found when I was looking for my ledgers. Mmm, the bread smells good Judith. Let's have something to eat and after we can sit here as it's nice and warm, and have a look at something I have found in this book. You will be very interested in its Pietro,' she said smiling.

Later she read from the book. 'Vigilantius was a Spaniard and taught the pure un-adulterated beliefs that were originally taught at the school of the 'Apostle John.' These people were the original early Christians, before the Roman church. Their teaching reached the then-known world and they retired in the 'Italian Alps' at Bobbio Pellice during persecution in the second, third and fourth centuries.

Then there was Columbanus, who was part of the first French Celtic Church. He also set up many churches and training colleges, fleeing to Switzerland, and then he retired to Bobbio where he set up the Intellectual Centre of Learning. He died in 615 in Bobbio.

'Now this part will interest you,' she said looking up at Pietro. 'Your ancestor was Baron Peter Waldo. His real French name was de Vaux. This is where the Vaudois name came from. He owned a castle in Lyons, France. One day while attending a conference at St Peter's, his best friend suddenly died. It upset him so much that he started searching the scriptures. He went back to the Pope and the cardinals with the Bible truths he found. The Pope declared that under no circumstance was he to preach and spread his knowledge. He continued to preach, setting up 'the poor men of Lyon,' who took the oath of poverty and worked for the poor. He also retired in the mountains of Italy in the eleventh century.'

SEVERAL WEEKS LATER, Pietro was pruning trees in the olive orchard. The last of the crop had been harvested several weeks earlier and the season was well past. Pietro stretched and thankfully accepted the water, offered by Judith. It was an overcast day with gusty winds. Winter was approaching, and soon it would be snowing. Judith pulled her shawl closer and returned to the kitchen.

In the far distance, a lone figure sat on a cart, pulled by a mule. Pietro recognized instantly who it was. It was his father. Throwing down his tools he ran through the olive orchard towards the far lane, to meet him.

'Papa, Papa,' he called and waved as the cart pulled into 'Valli di Dio.' His father jumped down as Pietro ran down the lane towards him, and they fell into each other's arms.

CHAPTER 9

FLAGELLANTS

*P*ietro pulled the ropes tighter around their packed cart's covering. Signora had gifted farm products and clothing. After many hugs, Judith and John de Vaux climbed onto the cart as old Leo and Jeanne watched and waved goodbye from the barn's outer door. Pietro, who was accompanying Judith and his father part of the way, mounted his horse and waved to Signora, Jeanne, and Leo.

'Don't forget to visit the next time you are passing this way. God be with you on your travels,' Signora called as the cart moved away.

'Grazie, Arrivèderci,' Pietro called, walking his horse beside the cart.

'I will never forget your kindness,' Judith said weeping as she waved.

The mule walked steadily on, as their little cart bumped along the rocky tracks. They were hoping to get to Alessandria before nightfall.

They passed ploughed fields and trees in the orchards waving their bare branches. The sheep huddled together against the autumn winds.

Judith sat with her cloak hood well over her head. They passed through an open valley, then up a steep incline. Over the other side, they entered a dense woody grove that became dark and gloomy, intensifying the cold winds.

The mule jerked to a stop. They looked up, and there they were, dangling practically in their faces. Dead bodies hung from trees. There were men, women, and children. The trees were filled with them. They hung like decorations, terrible decorations. The valley reeked with a putrefied stench.

A scream rent the air and echoed through the woods. Over and over again the sound pierced the silence, sending spine-tingling shivers up Father's back. Then all was quiet with only the restless sighing of the wind through the trees.

As the terrifying screams echoed through the woods, Pietro scouting ahead reined in his horse and listened. *'That's Judith screaming. It sounds like they went in another direction.'* He felt an icy chill run through his veins. *'I must quickly find them.'* Pietro turned his horse and galloped in the direction of the screams. Soon he saw the cart in the dense part of the woods.

Judith buried her head into father de Vaux's chest. The old mule took fright and snorted and stamped under its load, but was restrained by father.

Pietro galloped towards the cart. *'What's that,'* he thought as something above touched his head. He looked up to see a foot dangling in his face. Pietro caught his breath. '*Dead people hanging in the trees, what's going on? The smell, it's horrid. It makes me feel sick. They have been here for days judging by the stench,*' he thought.

He rode up to his father and spoke. 'This doesn't look like the work of papal soldiers as they are more likely to stake or burn their victims.'

'Actually, it looks like the work of 'Flagellants,' Father replied, placing his finger to his lips. He nodded towards Judith with her head down, clinging to his arm. Her lips were moving as she silently prayed.

'Si, I have heard about these overzealous misinformed

people,' Pietro replied. 'They march from town to town, usually in groups of two to three hundred people, all wearing red crosses on their white clothes. Often, they camp in fields near towns.' Pietro now looked around, fear creeping over his whole being. 'Save us please Lord Jesus,' he prayed out loud.

'Amen' Judith's trembling voice muttered into father's cloak.

Looking around father now reasoned. 'We are nearing Alessandria. Usually, large numbers of people flock around Flagellants when they visit towns. We must be very careful. Let's stop here and change into the clothes Signora has given us. They will recognize us as Waldenses in our normal clothes. They consider us to be troublemakers of the state.'

The men quickly changed into Signora's deceased husband's clothes, while Judith still shivering with fear, sat mournfully in the cart.

'Don't worry Judith, we should be in Alessandria soon and you will be able to rest at our friend, Paul Geymarli's home. Here, takes this warm wool cloak that Signora has given you.' Pietro tenderly wrapped it around her shoulders. 'Signora bought this cloak in Milano, the fashion centre of Italy. It is well worn but in keeping with the 'gentry' of this area,' he gently explained.

Soon they came out of the woods into open fields. The sun shone through the grey patchy clouds, making the distant dome glow on Alessandria's Cathedral.

SEVERAL HOURS LATER they approached the gates on the city's western wall, to find themselves surrounded by a huge crowd moving out of the city.

'I wonder what's happening,' father remarked.

'Look over there by the wall,' Pietro said, as he nodded towards a group of strange-looking people, stripped to their waists, marching around in a circle. The town folk pushed closer and watched noisily with much cheering and gesturing. The marching men flung themselves to the ground. In a crouched position they began to beat themselves with whips. Two boys watching pretended to whip each other, twisting their faces in pain; the others whooped in admiration.

'See that? Judith gasped cringing. They are whipping themselves with sticks with three knotted thongs hanging from the end.'

Pietro nodded towards the whips. 'Si and look at the metal piece in the middle. It looks like a cross. That part of the whip will cause the most damage. See how quickly they are bruising themselves. Some are making their bodies quite swollen.'

The Flagellants whipped themselves into a wild frenzy, calling out to God. 'God have mercy on us. God remove the plagues from the homes in this city. God, we have destroyed the cursed Jews and Jewish people for you. Your wrath is brought down upon us in the form of plagues because of their witchcraft. They have caused the plague to come upon us, even though they stay free from this dread disease,' they shouted as they whipped themselves, spraying their blood upon the city's wall.

'How sad it is to watch these deluded people,' father said, shaking his head. 'If only they knew, that Jesus doesn't expect them to do such penance. He forgave us all when he died on the cross. How evil the outcome has been from such delusions?'

Judith, white with fear, leaned closer to Pietro, as he walked his horse by the side of the cart. She spoke in a whisper. 'Pietro, they blame us for the plague. Did they kill all those people in the woods?'

'Si, when the plague approaches, they turn up with their rituals and encourage the locals to join them in their death frenzies, killing whole Jewish and Waldensian communities. They say we are poisoning their wells. They don't realize their sewage pits are near their wells and are contaminating their drinking water. This is causing sickness and death.'

Turning the mule's head towards the open city gate, Father looked over his shoulder and spoke to Pietro who was now behind the cart. 'Let's move into the city and to our friend Paul's home while everyone is busy and not watching us.'

They entered the gates on the west side of the city, which was the poorer side, with hovels closely clustered together against the wall. The old ladies came out of these doorways, swathed in heavy cloaks of coarse wool, and went down to the river to fetch water for the evening meal. Now and again, they would glance towards the commotion outside the city walls.

Their cart turned a corner into the piazza, which was bordered by shops. Across from the avenue of trade was the city's huge cathedral in all its glory. It sat high on paved stairways, yawning down with superior indifference upon all residing there. Here young boys', who were forbidden to join the mob, squatted on its porch, scratching themselves and spitting on the ground. They talked with studied confidence about the hangings in the woods.

One said, 'Dying like that can take the time a man takes to walk a mile.'

Another said, 'It could be worse than that, I have seen one, and before the man died his neck was so long his feet hit the ground and he tried to run.'

'Haw, haw, haw, stupid,' they called, as they ran down the church stairs.

The sun had set and the buildings now cast shadows across the market square. Small silhouettes darted in and out of the shadows and their voices echoed as they shouted back and forth.

'I'll beat you home,' one shouted.

'No, you won't. I can run faster than you.'

'Catch me if you can,' responded the other.

In the market piazza, the shop windows with their exotic wares were now in darkness. They passed these closed shops, with their upstairs candle lights flickering behind shutters. These stately substantial stone buildings graced the town's cobbled square. They were similar to Signora's country home, with a central courtyard and the living rooms above with shops below.

Pietro pulled on the bell rope outside the large wooden doors. The doors flung open with Paul standing there.

'Come in my good friends. You must be tired and hungry. We were so worried about you, with the rituals going on outside the gate,' he said hugging each of them as his servant led their cart and mule, plus the horse to the stables. 'Did you hear about the terrible so-called 'cleansing killings?' he asked.

'We saw the results hanging in the forest,' Pietro replied, shuddering.

After dinner, Judith retired early and the men gathered in the drawing room around a large fire, discussing the day's events.

The conversation turned from murder and the Flagellants to the plague, which was on the minds of all present. Pietro explained the new medical measures to stop the advancement of the Black Plague.

'This time around, the plague hasn't had the same devastating effect as it did one hundred years ago. People are more aware of health measures, and they seem to have inherited a stronger resistance to the disease, well the gentry certainly has. We are seeing well-run hospitals in the larger cities for those who can afford them, with good nursing care that allows the patients to rest and have proper nutrition. I'm not sure about the poor in their closely settled, rundown hovels and streets. It seems in these areas we are experiencing the outbreaks, and of course in the poor people's country cottages.'

The front bell clanged loudly downstairs and the butler answered it. A few minutes later two young men stood in the doorway of the drawing room.

'Enzo and Carlo I am so glad you have made it safely,' Paul said, as he stood and went to the door to shake their hands. 'Come in and meet our visitors.'

'John and Pietro, I wish to introduce you to your countrymen, who have been helping us save the Waldenses in this city,' and before he could continue, Pietro stepped forward laughing.

'Well, well, well, we meet again,' he said as he hugged the visitors. He turned to Paul and explained. 'Enzo and Carlo are friends from Torre Pellice. We spent the winter months together in the school of the Barbs, and then we went to the University at Firenze to study medicine.'

Father John de Vaux stepped forward shaking their hands with back-slapping and laughter.

Sitting in front of a warm fire, the conversation took on a personal level, reminiscing on past adventures, school, village life, and the attacks on the mountain folk.

Paul, a tall elegant merchant, stood and stepped up to the hearth and held out his hands to warm himself as he spoke. 'These attacks have become a full onslaught on the Waldensian people by the Pope and the kings. If that isn't bad enough also the common folk, have joined in, across the whole world. It certainly is Armageddon. All your people will perish if the Lord doesn't soon return.'

CHAPTER 10

PLAGUE

The next morning Pietro found Judith sitting in the court garden. She held the handwritten scriptures that he had given her and was quietly reading and praying.

'Buongiorno Judith. Papa is ready.' He held his hand out to her. As she rose, the sadness in her eyes, made it nearly impossible for him to say goodbye. He gently drew her to himself and held her close. He felt the babe kick within her. In his Patois tongue, he spoke softly. 'You will be safe with my family, and this summer you will have your little one, and I should be home by then.'

'Si,' she answered between wrenching sobs.

'Pietro, Judith, we must leave as it's a long journey,' father called.

Pietro stood at the front door waving to his father and Judith, who continually wiped her eyes. At that moment he felt homesick, very alone and frightened, and remembering the conversation the night before he thought, *'What am I doing away from home and my loved ones?'*

PIETRO FELT A TAP on his shoulder. He turned and then jumped back. A 'Black Bird' was standing behind him. Laughing dark-eyed, curly-haired Enzo, whose family originated from Rome, pulled off his headgear.

Pietro laughed, 'Where did you get the medical drapes?'

'Doctor Solomon Michelini left them here for us to use, if and when the plague approached the city,' Enzo said, with eyes rolling in a mocking gesture.'

'Is he nearby?' asked Pietro hopefully.

'Si, si, but he's gone to Milano, and will be back in a few weeks,' Enzo explained with palms up, grinning and nodding.

Carlo walked towards them in his 'Black Bird' outfit, holding there's in his arms. 'Here's your gown and mask, Pietro. Let's get going, we'll not clean up the city chatting.'

The early morning mist hung over the city, and roosters that perched along the city's wall trumpeted the first light of day. Old bent women hugging their shawls quietly moved to the river edge collecting water to boil on their fires. Enzo, Carlo, and Pietro, in their 'Black Bird' medical cloaks and masks walked down the narrow lanes discussing the procedures they were going to take.

'Si,' continued tall skinny Carlo, with his large floppy moustache, now hidden under his mask. 'Paul has organized men with carts to pick up the dead, and carpenters to board up the hovels, so those living with the dead stay confined in their hovels. Also, see those three young men over there? The pots they are carrying have red paint in them. They will follow us, and place crosses on the doors of the afflicted, so no one will enter. Also, this will help the carpenters to recognize the diseased dwellings. They should be here at any moment. Let's separate and go individually to all the cottages and we must move quickly before the people take flight.'

As they passed by in their 'Black Bird' outfits, young children screamed and ran to their mothers. The old signoras looked up, crossed themselves, muttered, and hurried into their hovels, slamming the doors behind them.

'Has God sent demons to punish us?' one small boy whispered.

'No,' replied his mother. 'They are 'Black Birds' sent by God to help us.'

Suddenly a man screamed, and all heads jerked in his direction. His whole face was swollen and red and his left eye was closed. A large red lump rose above his eye while they watched. He ran to the city's gates, but they were closed.

On the wealthier side of the town's square, Paul Geymarali's wife locked herself in her room above their shop, biting her fingernails to the quick. Paul feared she would lose her mind. She hunched into a ball and wept. 'God where are you?' she called.

The death carts pulled into the narrow laneways. People panicked and ran to and fro screaming. 'The plague is coming. The plague is already here.'

A young mother ran through the streets. Her hair had turned white overnight. She held her dead child in her arms as she ran.

'Open the gates,' Pietro screamed, 'and let these people out. Don't let them back in or they will infect the whole city.'

Going from hovel to hovel, Pietro, Carlo, and Enzo instructed the families. As they watched, swellings rose in armpits, groins, and necks. Fear overtook modesty and the people pulled off their clothes for examination.

Pietro examined the buboes without touching the infected people. 'Please apply a warm poultice of onion or garlic on the swellings,' he encouraged the afflicted. 'It may draw out the infection.'

It was now mid-day and the stench of death lodged in

their nostrils and the screams of the living rang in their ears. Bodies of the dead piled up in the streets.

Among the activities, the thudding of hammers nailing up the hovels of the diseased echoed through the polluted air. With every hammer stroke, people stopped and listened to the screams of families trapped in the barricaded dwellings. Terrified, they were willing to desert their afflicted family members and escape, but this wasn't to be. All in contact with those afflicted had to be imprisoned in their homes until the disease took their family members and more than likely them also. If fortunate they may be amongst those who recover and are set free.

The cries of abandoned babies rose in the air as Pietro, Carlo, and Enzo in their 'Black Bird' cloaks, walked past the boarded hovels. They were helpless. This was not an enemy they could see or run from. Under his mask, Pietro's tears washed his face and he was glad that no one could see his reaction.

'Lord Jesus, how terrible these deeds are. But what can we do Lord? The plague will take the whole city if we don't isolate the infected people. How wretched I feel. I can hardly contain my sorrow. If I feel this way, how much more You and Your angels must be stricken by this sin-sick world? You have given us 'health laws but man has turned from you and your ways.

Enzo and Carlo also struggled with their feelings and the enormity of this dread plague. Loud sniffing took place behind Enzo's mask, and then he coughed pretending he had a cold, but they all knew he was crying.

They tried to reason with the people standing outside the hovels. Pietro spoke to them. 'You can take food to them; pass it through the gaps in the boards. You must not touch those inside or bring out any utensils. When you have completed your delivery, you must scrub your hands with soap and vinegar in a bowl of water. The water must not be emptied on the ground or in the river but down the city's toilet pits. When all the sick have died in the dwellings you must let the men with the carts know. They will take the boards down and remove their bodies. After one week, family members must go in and scrub the dwelling with soap and vinegar and burn all the clothes within. You must burn immediately your clothes, worn while carrying out these duties. If a family member survives, they must stay boarded up in the dwelling until they are examined.'

The sun now dipped towards the hills and the streets cooled suddenly as the light faded. At sunset, the living entered the Cathedral for evening prayers. A hum of voices rose amongst the flickering candles as they prostrated themselves in supplication. 'Please God deliver us. Please deliver your children.' Most people thought the plague was punishment from God for their sins.

CHAPTER 11

PAUL'S HELP

Many days later, when all that could be done for the afflicted people in Alessandria was done, Pietro, Carlo, and Enzo rode their horses out to the countryside. They were anxious to see how folk on their small holdings survived the plague. They sheltered under a large oak while heavy rain soaked the ground. Pietro was glad for his mother's thick warm cloak, and after all, it had Bible verses hidden in the lining, and these could be shared with the sick.

'We need to get on with the task at hand, before the cold sets in. Our clothes are wet and if we get chilled, we could become sick,' Pietro said. 'Let's go in different directions. We can do it quicker if we separate. There may be folk still alive and needing our assistance. Let's meet here at sunset.'

He took a sharp turn to the left and headed towards open pastures. Soon he came across a farm and was shocked to see a whole family lying dead near their well. Neighbouring farms were deserted. Cattle wandered around without herdsmen. He passed barns and wine cellars with their doors standing wide open. There were hardly any people to be found. Bodies laid by the side of the road. Flies buzzed around these dead bodies, and rain washed their vomit down the dirt track. Riding quickly passed the scene Pietro came to another small farm and watched warily for movement from a man lying by the cottage's doorway. The man ever so slightly moved his hand. Jumping from his horse Pietro knelt by his side to assist him. The man lifted his head and looked past Pietro. He started to moan. Footsteps approached from behind but Pietro didn't hear them, because of the moaning. The moaning turned into a loud howl. It seemed to go on and on. Suddenly there was a hard thud on Pietro's head and then there was nothing.

Opening his eyes, there was a swirl of movement. Pietro's head throbbed and he winced in pain. Light from flaming torches fluttered in front of him. Excruciating pain seared through the nerves behind his eyes. He winced as a rope passed over his face, scraping on the cuts on the back of his head. that were bleeding profusely *Who are these people?* He thought.

People erupted on every side. They moved closer.

'I'm in the forest, amongst the dead bodies hanging from trees, and the stink is even more putrid than a few days earlier.' Pietro thought.

The Flagellants in their white gowns with red crosses danced and sang around him in a threatening frenzy.

'I am about to be hung,' Pietro thought.

The man that was in front of the cottage's door, was now grinning at him, showing his yellow teeth that shone like ivory in the torch light.' It's your turn to go to hell, young preacher of heresy,' he spat.

The crowd cheered.

Pietro looked up through the tree's dark shadowy branches at the starry sky and prayed. *'Lord, be with me, please. I trust you, Lord, let it not be my will but your will dear Jesus. Amen.'*

The man stood back and yanked on the rope. The noose dug deep into Pietro's throat and he gasped as air was instantly blocked. Thumping in his throat pulsated in time with his heart. Pain from lack of oxygen seared through his brain. He now became dizzy, and all seemed far away. Then another thudding could be heard. Suddenly a shoulder was under him and a hand loosened the rope around his throat. A blade was felt, and the rope choking him was cut. His body sank onto a horse, as arms held him, and now free from the rope he sucked in ragged breaths.

Quick movements followed as the man and his horse moved forward with Pietro abreast. Flagellant people grabbed at the horse, also Pietro and the rider.

The sound of many horses galloping toward Pietro and his rider could be heard. Suddenly the man holding back the horse was thrown off his feet as a sharp dagger impacted his chest. Moaning he died. Soldiers galloped amongst the crowd, brandishing their swords, and many more people died. Their frenzied singing now became screaming. Suddenly the people of the forest disappeared into the darkness of the night.

On horseback Paul Geymarli and the Sheriff's men surrounded Pietro. Carefully they lowered him onto a cart. Pietro lay under skins, his breath still jagged. He was very glad of the softness under his throbbing head. He felt for his mother's cloak that held the precious Bible verses.

'Si,' he thought, *I am still wearing my cloak. They didn't know about the hidden tracts, so that's good. Someone had told them about me being a Waldense because* they *were following my movements.'*

Staring up at the sky, now covered with clouds that threatened to rain, he prayed.

'*Lord my prayer was answered before I prayed. You had these people already in place to save me, thank you Lord for your great love. In Jesus' name Amen.'*

THE NEXT MORNING Pietro lay in his bed listening to his friends' voices in the kitchen below. He slowly stood and painfully dressed. It was too much for him to stay upstairs away from all that was happening. *'I must go down,* he thought. *'How did they know where to go last night?* He mused. He slowly took the stairs, one at a time, groaning with each step.

Carlo heard his groans and looked out the kitchen door. 'Well look who's here. The walking dead,' he chuckled. 'Here let me help you, my friend,' he said as he placed an arm around Pietro and walked him to a chair next to the kitchen fire.

'How did you know where to find me?' Pietro asked.

Carlo looked at Enzo and recounted the events. 'We waited at the oak tree, as agreed. It was getting dark and sunset had passed and you hadn't returned so we knew something was very wrong.'

'Si, si' butted in Enzo, 'we did this. We waited, but we knew something was very wrong as you're such a stickler for time.'

Carlo continued, 'We rode our horses in the direction you took and came across a signor with his cart full of furs. His name was Elio. He was sitting in his cart hugging his cloak over his tunic. We knew something was wrong, but it was dark and we couldn't see properly. He told us he had gone to the back door of Angelo the trader's home, to sell furs to him.

Enzo excitedly joined in, 'Si, si, that's right. While standing at the door, Elio with the cart had a sword pushed against his ribs by someone behind the door. The owner of the home, the trader, was tied and gagged inside, you know,' he threw his arms around and paced the floor.

'Si,' continued Carl, 'The stranger behind the door was one of those Flagellant people. He held a sword and with its tip he nudged Elio, the signor with the cart into the room, causing him to fall to the floor. Blood dripped down his belly from the jab, and seeped through his tunic. The Flagellant thought he was dead and left quickly with the others, who were dragging you away. We knew where they would be taking you, so we rode back to Paul Geymarali's place, and Paul brought the Sheriff.'

Enzo who was still pacing finished the story, with a lot of hand gesturing. 'Si, si, Elio, the signor with the cart went straight to the forest, bleeding and all.' He said with hands on his belly and eyes rolling. He continued, 'We passed him as we entered the forest.'

Pietro croaked, 'Is the signor with the cart, alright?

'Si, si, the wound was very small,' Enzo said using his fingers to show how small with lots of nodding.

'And the hunter?' Pietro enquired.

'Si, si, he's alright,' Enzo said, nodding his head.

'Well praise the lord, that you were on time,' Pietro croaked and coughed.

A hearty slap on the back was given to Pietro by the well-meaning Enzo. Pietro winced.

Paul entered with his family's handwritten Bible and placed the heavy book on the kitchen table. 'Let's pray and then study the scriptures here by the warm fire,' he suggested. All knelt in gratitude that God had spared Pietro's life.

SEVERAL DAYS LATER the youth were ready to leave for Firenze. Paul's servant held open the courtyard's large heavy door, as they rode through to the cobbled street beyond.

'Arrivèderci and Grazie for all your hard work,' Paul called, 'don't forget to come again.

'Arrivèderci,' they responded.

CHAPTER 12

STRANGER IN THE NIGHT

*I*n the dawn's silence a cock's crow reverberated through the morning mist, joined by the echoing click-clack of their horses' hooves on the cobbled street, as they passed out the city gates.

Pietro sighed as he looked around at the mist-covered forest beyond and then back at the city's walls. 'Praise the Lord the plague isn't as bad as it was a hundred years ago. I was told in some areas, over eighty percent of the population perished. This time it seems to be attacking the poorer areas and then mostly the young, sick, and old.'

They sat on their horses and looked over the valley, and rolling hills. Mist blanketed the landscape like a carpet. Pietro pulled his mother's cloak closer around his shoulders.

Carlo astride his horse sat contemplating, as he twisted the edge of his long droopy moustache with the fingers of his left hand.

'Do you think we could get to Bobbio by nightfall? I believe it is a good day's journey from here,' he said.

Pietro thought about the name and responded. 'It's strange that we have two Bobbios, one in the mountains where we come from, and one down here.'

Nodding Enzo agreed, 'Si and it too is a Waldensian stronghold. It will be good to spend time there with our brethren.

Pietro now thought of Judith and his father. *'It's been nearly two weeks since they left. They should be nearly home. I wonder if it's snowing in the mountains,'* he thought.

Enzo nudged his horse to a gallop. 'Well let's get going,' he called back to them, looking over his shoulder with a wicked grin, as they quickly galloped up to him. He then continued. 'Si, si, that's right move it, Signors. I have a young Signorina I would like to visit, as soon as we get there.'

After some time, they entered a forest. They became apprehensive and cautiously looked around to see if Flagellant people were hiding amongst the trees.

Enzo started singing at the top of his voice. The others laughed at their foolishness and joined in.

> *God's peace be with you,*
> *All the days of your life*
> *No one will stand*
> *Against you in strife,*
> *Wherever you go,*
> *God will take care of you.'*

They came out through the other side of the forest, to rolling hills, fields, and farmers attending their land. Then they rode through villages with town folk about their business, and back out into the countryside, where small boys herded their cattle homeward. It was now late afternoon and the sun dipped behind the hills. They ascended a rise and there it was, Bobbio, a small city surrounded by high walls.

Carlo pointed. 'Look is that smoke coming from the city's piazza?'

Pulling up their horses, they stared in the direction where

Carlo pointed.

'Si, si, and by the look of it, lots of smoke,' Enzo replied, throwing his hands out wide while still holding his horse's reins. The horse jerked its head back and it snorted and reared up, nearly tossing Enzo to the ground.

Carlo lent forward to steady the horse. 'How long did you say you have been riding?' he asked laughing.

Pietro galloped off. 'I'm going to see what's going on,' he shouted.

The others followed. As they approached the city they could see soldiers, guarding the gates. Pietro realized with a shock, what he had led his friends into.

'It's the papal legate Cataneo's soldiers. They have been slaughtering the Waldensian people throughout the region and by the looks of things, here also. We are in big trouble if they see us. Let's get out of here,' he said, and quickly turned his horse and galloped away before they were noticed, and the others followed.

They rode through neighbouring fields and Carlo who was at the rear looked back at the city. 'I hate to tell you this, Amico's but Cataneo and his troop have just passed through the city's gate and are heading this way.'

Enzo with eyes wide with fear responded, and once again jerked his horse. 'Si, si, he is Pietro, what shall we do?'

Pietro noticed a man in the field forking hay from his cart to his cattle and galloped across to him. 'Please Signor, can we take shelter for a short while in your stables.'

The man slowly looked Pietro up and down. 'Si,' he thought to himself, *'A Waldensian youth and the army is heading this way.'* He nodded. 'When you get there take off your packs and place the horses with mine and hide all your

75

things and yourselves in the hay,' he said.

'Grazie Signor,' Pietro replied.

When they placed their horses with the man's, Carlo spoke. 'Let's change into those clothes you were given, Pietro. If they find us, they will think we are local travellers, and because of our years at college we can copy their brogue if they speak to us.'

'Si, si, good idea, but it's too late because they are nearly here,' Enzo squeaked, and with that he jumped into the hay, pushing it over him, and the others quickly followed.

The army travelled along a small lane-way that passed right beside the stables. Cataneo at the front of his troop stopped for a moment and looked in. He saw only horses, so he and his men rode on.

The blue sky had turned dark grey. It was twilight and nearly dark. Pietro and Enzo were brushing hay off themselves and Carlo was attending to the horses when the farmer appeared.

'Amico's, it's too late to ride on. I have brought you some bread and cheese for supper. Sleep here until morning. The army will pass by later this evening so find a spot where they won't see you,' he advised.

Lying on the straw they recited Bible verses that they learned as children. It rained through the night and Pietro listened to its pelting vibrations on the barn's roof.

He prayed, *Father in heaven I thank you for your wonderful care and love towards us. It is difficult for me to be amongst such cruelty, but Lord daily I see your protection. I wish Lord to do your will and to spread your word. Please give me the courage to continue with this work, in such a dark world. My heart is sad and so weary. Our Brethren in Bobbio have been attacked. Be with them in their last hour. Comfort and encourage them to be strong in You. This I pray in Jesus' name, Amen.*

THEY ROSE EARLY in the morning. The sky was bluish grey, with patchy dark clouds that threatened to rain. The path was soddened with large puddles. The day was long, and as they rode each was deep in thought.

They came to a small village that was completely deserted, and the silence was eerie. The only sound to be heard was the thudding of shop doors, which were left wide, open, to swing back and forth in the wind. The shops' shelves were turned over and produce spilt across the floors. Rats scurried around busy in their newfound freedom. Dogs were eating meat from the butcher's stand. The cottages on the edge of the village were empty. Where were all the people? Not a sound could be heard. Cattle unattended walked across the lane to the nearby fields.

'Si over there,' Enzo pointed.

And there it was. The cruellest form of torture had taken place. The whole village, men, women, children and babies had long metal stakes shoved through the length of their bodies. They hung in a terrible line along the edge of the pathway. Agony, terrible agony, was depicted on their frozen dead features.

'I wonder who passed through this village?' Carlo asked.

'It would have been soldiers passing through. This would have been a great sport for them.' Pietro explained.

Enzo swung his horse around and rode from the scene. The others followed in grim silence.

They let their horses have their heads and rode harder and faster than ever before. Enzo rode, lying flat down on his mount with his head close to its neck, yipping to it, making it gallop even faster. Carlo also leaned right down for speed, shaking his head like he had a nervous twitch. Pietro with the wind on his face, and eyes filled with tears, didn't notice a young herd's boy, who almost darted under his horse.

All were disgusted at what they saw. They rode until the sun sank low in the sky, and then they stopped at a creek to rest and wipe their horses' foaming bodies. They must get them dry before nightfall, as it was gusty and cold. Gathering sticks, they lit a fire and turned to their Savior for peace. They opened their handwritten Bible verses and read them out loud by the light of the fire.

Enzo led out in the Lord's Prayer, 'Our Father which is in Heaven.' The others joined in, and then another voice, soft and harmonious behind them could be heard. They swung around to find a tall stranger standing there praying with them. They kept on until they finished, all the while keeping a good eye on the stranger who continued to recite the Lord's Prayer with them.

'Please join us,' Pietro offered.

The stranger nodded and sat on a log by the fire. He continued to wear his hood low over his forehead and held his head down. His dark cloak was very different from anything they had seen. He wore sandals and looked to be as poor as they were. When he spoke, his voice was warm and soft. 'I wish to encourage you with the work you are doing. All heaven is watching. To share the written word is the only way to show the truth to your deceived countrymen. Do you realize that in the early centuries the Bible was written in many, many different languages and was spread across the world? Then the papal system was set up with man-made rules, and death penalties were put in place to stamp out the Celtic Christians'

All three sat still wondering who their new friend was. Carlo twisted both edges of his moustache with his fore-fingers and thumbs, as was his habit when concentrating. The stranger wasn't local as he spoke with a different brogue, and he certainly wasn't a papal soldier.

He continued, 'In a far-off continent called England a man called Wycliffe while at college found the fountain of truth in the Bible. He dedicated himself to the service of Christ and was determined to proclaim the truths he had discovered.

Wycliffe was a keen detector of error, and he stood fearlessly against many of the abuses sanctioned by the authority of Rome. While he was acting as chaplain to the king of England, he took a bold stand against the payment of tribute, claimed by the Pope from the English monarch, and showed that the papal assumption of authority over secular rulers was contrary to reason.

Wycliffe was appointed as a royal ambassador of England, and spent two years in the Netherlands, in conference with the commissioners of the Pope. Here he was brought into communication with the religious leaders from France, Italy, and Spain, and he had an opportunity to look behind the scenes and gain knowledge of many things which would have remained hidden from him in England. In these representatives from the papal court, he read the true character and aims of the hierarchy. He returned to England declaring that covetousness, pride, and deception were the gods of Rome. In one of Wycliffe's tracts he wrote, 'the papacy took the poor's livelihoods, and many thousand marks, of the king's money, for sacraments and spiritual things, which is a cursed practice, keeping the church rich and the nation poor.

When he returned to England Wycliffe received from the king, his appointment to the rectory. He knew through this that the King wasn't displeased with him, but it was a different matter in Rome. They knew he could influence the king against them. The papal thunders were soon hurled against him. Three bulls were dispatched to the king to silence the teacher of heresy.' He held his hands over the fire and rubbed them together, and continued with his story; a story that came from a far country.

Was he a travelling missionary? Pietro wondered.

The stranger went on with his story. 'The reformer continued with his work. The same as your people have been doing for hundreds of years; writing the Bible in your native tongue for all to hear, and for those that can, read. Wycliffe also placed the Bible, the most powerful of all weapons against Rome, in the hands of his people. It was the first English translation ever made. The word of God was opened to England. In giving the Bible to his countrymen, he had done more to break the fetters of ignorance and vice, more to liberate and elevate his country, than ever achieved by the most brilliant victories on the battlefields. The English King gave him protection while he completed his work, and Wycliffe died a short while later. The Pope never had a chance to carry out his death threats.'

He stopped and took the mug of hot drink that Pietro offered him. Sipping the drink, he continued.

'Now I must tell you about two other faithful men, Huss

and Jerome. John Huss was from Bohemia and of humble birth. He won a charity scholarship to go to the University of Prague and was a sincere adherent of the Roman Church. After completing his scholarship, he entered the priesthood and was appointed preacher in the Chapel of Bethlehem. While presiding over the church, he realized there was widespread ignorance of the Bible, and the worst vices prevailed amongst the people of all ranks because of this. Si,' he nodded to them, as they listened intently to him. 'That's right he started to share the scriptures with his congregation.

Increasing in boldness, Huss thundered against the abominations which were tolerated. He faithfully showed his people Biblical truths. He was brought many times before the council but continued with his work. The last time Huss was brought before the council, they decided to burn him at the stake.

The other young man named Jerome was a citizen from Prague, and when he returned to Bohemia from England, he brought with him Wycliffe's writings and joined Huss in the work of reform. For sharing the Bible truths with his people, Jerome was imprisoned for twelve months, and later put on the stake and burned to death. So, you can see with these stories, many others in far-off lands are also witnessing and suffering persecution.'

The stranger now stood, and as he drew his cloak closer, he said. 'All heaven has witnessed the great work your people have undertaken over the seasons of time. The seeds have been scattered, and the truth will triumph. All heaven rejoices at your faithfulness. Others are taking up the call. Be fortified true and faithful witnesses; your endurance and patience honour your Redeemer.' He then walked into the night.

'Did you see that?' Enzo said with eyes boggling. 'Look at that,' he said waving his hands. 'He has vanished. Si, si, there isn't anyone out there.' They all looked across the open fields. The sky was clear and the moon bright, and all was still. The fields were completely void of all movement. Enzo continued. 'It was an angel sent to comfort us. How good our Lord is?' He now wept tears of joy.

CHAPTER 13

FIRENZE

Florence Cathedral Santa Maria

The next day they rode through Tuscany's autumn landscape, with olive orchards and sprawling bare vineyards that now had a sprinkling of snow. Magnificent gardens surrounded the grand villas, which were perched like sentinels on the rolling hills.

Towards evening, they traversed the mountains, riding their tired mounts slowly up a steep incline, and there it was, Firenze, the capital of the world. It left them breathless with its size and grandeur. Sitting on their mounts they looked across the river Arno.

Pietro pointed across the river, to the centre of the city. 'Let's see if we recognize the buildings from here,' he said and continued. 'The large red dome to the right is Santa Maria's Cathedral. See how it stands higher than all the other buildings in the city.

Enzo agreed with much nodding. 'Si, si it does,' he waved his hands in the direction of the building. 'It's much higher; you don't realize this when in the city. I will never forget the sight of this wonderful city,' he sighed.

Pietro continued with his commentary. 'The 'Santa Maria Cathedral,' is the largest brick building in the world and look you can see the top of the Baptistery building over there opposite Santa Maria.' He pointed in that direction. 'We must go to the tall tower over there.'

'Si, si, its 'Palace Vecchio,' Enzo responded.

Carlo turned and pointed to a large wooden bridge with lots of shops on its sidewalk and top of all the shops were windows running the length of the bridge. 'I will never forget that bridge it's the famous Ponte Vecchio.'

When they entered the bridge, its thoroughfare was narrow and people jostled on its walkway. They stepped down from their mounts and led them. They couldn't stop staring at the scene that passed before them. They had seen it many times before, but it always amused them.

Pietro nodded and whispered to Enzo. 'Look at the signoras, their fashions always change.'

Women were wearing heavy silk dresses from China. They were covered in large bold embossed pomegranate or artichoke motifs. The dresses had long sleeves and full skirts gathered under the bust. They looked like the fields beyond the city with their bright colours. But there were various styles of gowns worn, plus many different hairstyles and headdresses. Most of the fashionable signoras shaved the front of their heads and worn at the back of their heads, were turned back brims of fabric the same as their dresses, topped by a veil of fine white linen.

Enzo with mouth open stared at the garish sight that now passed before him. 'Look he whispered,' and nudged Pietro so hard, it nearly made him stumble. 'Did you see those signorina's?'

Pietro looked around to see young signorina in bright red velvet dresses hemmed with fur at the sleeves and neck, wearing their hair pulled to each side of their temples, fashioned to look like horns. Their veils were fastened behind these horns.

'Well, I think I have seen the devil himself,' Pietro whispered back.

Enzo shook his head trying not to laugh. 'Si, I think so.'

'Have you seen the shops?' Carlo asked when he caught up to them, nodding to the outside stalls. They all went closer, to stands filled with pure gold knick-knacks and jewellery of incredible designs.

Pietro shook his head at the latest designs and muttered. 'The wealth of this city never changes.'

They walked slowly, absorbing all they saw, and eventually they were on the other side of the bridge walking along the plaza Uffizi's thoroughfare with its shops nearly as spectacular as those on the bridge.

Carlo felt he could now talk. 'You do realize that the gold shops on the old bridge are owned and run by Jews? The Jews have been relegated to a few professions and pawnbroking is one of them. Also, substantial privileges have been granted to Jewish bankers. Lorenzo is a clever statesman and ruler. He realizes the talents of these people and the benefits he receives from them. Because of this, he is too wise to put anti-Semite acts in place,' Carlo explained. With his head down twisting one side of his moustache with his free hand, he now thought about the Jewish situation.

Pietro who had been studying a shop window turned to Carlo. 'Surely that's good for us, as we are classed as Jewish people. We may at long last have sanction while practising medicine in their advanced hospitals.'

Carlo nodded and continued, 'Si, but just remember that Duke Lorenzo's family the Medici's, are the Pope's bankers and the Pope will visit often. Also, this is the cultural centre of the world and because of this, it will draw the Pope and other leaders to the arts and festivals. We need to be very watchful at all times when we share the Bible truths.'

Soon they were standing in the square, looking at the

brass doors of the Baptistery. Cast into the brass, were wonderful Bible scenes.

People milling about the street stopped their activities and stared at a person approaching them, and then they bowed. It was Lorenzo, walking towards Pietro, Carlo, and Enzo on the Baptistery side, accompanied by his two aids.

He walked up to Pietro, Carlo, and Enzo with arms held out. 'One of my aids said you were on your way. Welcome to Firenze,' Lorenzo said and kissed the cheeks of all three. 'Please come with us to the hospital and I will personally show you your quarters.'

The gathering crowd stepped back in awe.

'The young men must be important,' one whispered.

'But they dress as commoners from a distant land,' commented another.

'Who can they be?' they whispered back and forth.

CHAPTER 14

IN THE MOUNTAINS

Judith and father crossed the plains from Pinerolo to Torre Pellice. The sky was grey and the wind gusty and cold. It blew down from the mountains and the trees bent their bare branches against its force. The women on the side of the track stumbled, adjusted their loads, and continued. The harvest was well over with only stubble evident across the fields. Judith pulled her cloak closer and hood further over her face. Large drops of rain fell on their shoulders, and then once again the clouds parted for a moment and the winter sun weakly shone. She was exhausted and was glad they were nearing home.

Father spoke, 'Well Judith we are nearly home. We have been on the road for two weeks. I am sorry, you must be so tired but we needed to visit the country cottages and the different village markets to trade produce and wares that we have carried back from the distant markets. But don't worry as my family know we are on our way.'

'Si, I understand,' Judith replied tiredly.

Several hours later they crossed the river at Torre Pellice and noticed women kneeling in their boxes, washing clothes on large slabs of slate. They had small fires near them, with large pots of water, which they used to warm their hands, as the river was freezing at this time of the year.

Sometime later their little cart, now nearly empty, pulled into the market square at Torre Pellice.

Father spoke, 'The market is nearly over. Families are

packing their carts' and readying themselves for the journey home to prepare the main meal of the day.'

A small dimpled child ran towards them. "Papa, Papa' we have been waiting for you,' she laughed, running into father's outstretched arms.

Soon, a solidly built woman with a winter bonnet and a pretty crocheted shawl tugged at his arm. 'John, you have nearly missed the market, but don't worry, I have folk organized to buy the fine woven materials and hand-tatted lace you've brought back from distant markets.' She smiled up at him, and it was easy for Judith to see the love they had for each other.

A solidly built youth, with brown curly hair and a dimpled chin that gave him a young angelic appearance, approached them. He nodded to Judith and turned to follow his father, and then stopped, turned, and stared at Judith. Suddenly the memory of the siege at Pinerolo came to him. His face burned with embarrassment. Shame engulfed him; shame for not helping her. He wanted to explain, wanted to say sorry, but he stuttered, and words wouldn't come.

Judith knew who he was. Pietro had explained to her, that his younger brother had witnessed the scene.

'It is alright Marco, Pietro has explained everything to me,' she said kindly.

Unbelievable relief came over Marco. The memory of what happened to her had been troubling him all this time, but now she was safe with them. He sighed, grinning in relief. Nodding to Judith he went to find his father, who was with the other traders.

His mother took Judith who had turned quite pale, by the arm. 'My name is Anna and I am Pietro's mamma. Come with me, dear. Maria and I are going ahead of the signors in our small carriage. It's getting late and far too cold to be standing around this empty market square. The signors will follow when they have finished their business.'

The ancient village of Borgata Cyrus is – 500 years old

Soon they were ascending the narrow pass. Higher, and higher they climbed into the mist. The track was dangerously close to the edge. Judith looked over the side and saw only mist.

Mother de Vaux holding the reigns tightly, continued to talk. 'I knew your parents. We often traded with them at the markets. We are very sorry for your loss, dear. You are most welcome to stay with our family especially as your bambino is on the way.'

'Grazie,' Judith replied shyly.

Soon they were at the family's village Borgata Cyrus and their mother de Vaux opened the large wooden doors to their small courtyard. Maria ran to the stables to let out her dog.

'Come, Mike, let's play,' she called as they ran down the village path.

Ascending the steps, Judith and Pietro's mother entered the main family room, with its large stone fireplace at one end.

'Let me show you our small home,' mother said. 'This is where we spend our time in winter.'

The room was long but cosy. Mother's cooking pot hung from a large chain over low embers. To one side was a brick oven. In front of the fireplace was a metal grate high enough to prevent sparks from leaping onto the floor or furniture beyond. A double bed stood between the hearth and the wall that ran along the covered verandah. At the end of the bed was a large chest for clothes. A small washstand with a jug and wash basin was nearby.

'This is yours and Maria's bed and as you can see, it will be a very cosy spot over the freezing months ahead,' she explained.

She took her through a large door to the other side of the hearth. The room ran along the second side of the building. It had a small wardrobe and dresser. Also, there was a wash table with a jug and basin. There was a large bed with its bed head pressed against the back of the fireplace. The stones even in this room were warm from the ever-lit kitchen fire in the other room.

'This is where we sleep in the winter,' mother explained.

'Downstairs is where Marco and Pietro when he's home,

sleep. They also sleep near the chimney in the winter months, as it's warm from the fire up here,' she explained.

Judith nodded but she felt exhausted. She held her stomach, a habit she had of late, partly because it was heavy, and partly because she liked to feel the baby move. It now kicked and turned over.

'Come dear you look tired. Let's have a nice warm mug of fresh milk, and then you can lie down and rest until the boys come home.'

When Judith was resting mother returned to the courtyard to take care of her horse and carriage. She could hear the men returning, and Maria could be heard talking excitedly over them. 'Papa Judith is going to live with us.'

'Young signorina be quiet, and Mike stop barking. Stop Mike. Do you hear me Mike stop?' demanded father, as the dog cowered down.

'Oh, dear what excitement,' mother muttered.

JUDITH SAT BY THE kitchen fire diligently plying the shuttle with its fine thread across her loom. *This thread Mamma de Vaux spun for me yesterday is lovely and soft. It will make nice swaddling clothes for my little one,'* she thought as she worked.

'Judith, Judith,' Maria called running into the room. 'Please come with me to the pastures, to collect our cow.'

Judith looked up and stretched.

'Please Judith,' Maria begged.

'Si, I need a break,' Judith replied. 'How cold is it out there?

'Very, and it has been snowing; just a tiny bit between the rain showers, but we will hold hands and you won't slip

Judith.'

'No, and you mustn't either,' Judith laughed. 'Wait and I will put on my cloak and you must put yours back on,' she advised Maria.

The snow was thin on the ground because of the rain, but Judith knew this would soon change. '*Those snow shoes hanging in the barn, we are going to need them in the next few days,*' she thought.

As they trudged to the far pasture, they passed Signora Duval and old Antonio Duval's cottage on the side of the mountain ridge. Blowing steam from their mouths they laughed and walked slowly, holding hands.

'Well, there she is,' Maria remarked, 'I can tell by the sound of her bell.'

'Si,' Judith agreed. 'By the look of that large patch of snow on the ground, she will be staying in her winter stables from today onwards.'

'Judith, can we visit Marco, just for a few minutes, at the Duval's? He's on watch, looking out for papal soldiers trying to sneak into our valleys.' She shuddered with the cold and clapped her gloved hands as she jumped up and down.

'Si, just for a few moments.'

Judith placed a rope around the cow's neck and they trudged down the hill singing. Maria tried to skip and nearly fell over and then decided to jump like a frog in time with the tune. Soon they were at Duval's cottage. Signora was waiting at the door.

'Be quick you two; you'll freeze me to death,' she shouted over their singing.

Quickly Judith tied the cow to the verandah and they stepped into the porch and removed their boots and cloaks.

Old Antonio handed them a hot drink. Marco didn't look around; he just stared out of the window.

'What are you looking at Marco?' Asked Maria going to the window. She also stared down the mountain pass. 'Marco someone is coming up the pass,' she said pointing.

'Si, and he's not one of us,' Marco replied.

All now rushed to the window.

'Blow your horn, Marco. Be quick, it's a Catholic monk,' shouted Signora Duval. 'Be quick; can't you find it,' she said as Marco rushed around the room, looking in all the corners and on the shelves.

'It's all right Marco,' old Antonio answered. 'I've found it.' He quickly went to the door and blew it with all his might. The sound vibrated through the valley and up and down the mountainside.

CHAPTER 15

A LONE MONK

Judith and Maria ran as fast as they could through the snow, with the cow trotting behind, while the horn echoed around them. Father ran to meet them. 'Quick go to Mamma,' he called as he ran to Duval's, pulling on his coat as he went.

Mother waited anxiously at the door. 'Quick, inside Maria, as we don't know how many there are,' she said.

Judith took the cow to the stables under the house and gave it hay, and rushed up the stairs to the living quarters, slamming and locking the door behind her.

'It's only a lone monk.' Maria explained, confused by all the anxiety.

THE MONK STOPPED, looked up, and listened. He knew they were warning each other of his approach, but trudged on. As he neared a corner on the narrow pass, men suddenly jumped out from the bushes and roughly grabbed him, knocking him to the ground.

'Take him to old Antonio's. That's where the watch is being held,' said the oldest of the three.

'Si, and by the look of the sky, we are in for heavy snow storms tonight. He will be trapped there for the whole winter,' another answered.

'Serves him right, as young Marco is on watch and he will give him good Bible lessons,' laughed the other.

The monk spoke Patois, and understood their speech, but

didn't realize the extent of the education he was about to receive; after all, the papacy was sending their preaching monks into the mountain valleys to teach the folk catholic traditions.

Men rushed through the snow from their family cottages. All were heading to the Duval's; some with instruments of war, others still pulling on coats or warm caps over their ears as they ran, but all were concerned over the fearful events that were occurring.

A babble of voices met the group, as they dragged the monk into Duval's cottage. Marco stood well back, pale and anxious with the event taking place, but he relaxed when he saw the old monk in his thin holey brown habit.

'I thought they were young, fat, and jolly, but this monk is thin, old, and has a worn expression,' Marco thought.

'Why have you come to our valley?' Father asked.

The monk spoke Patois in a tired, quiet voice. All present were surprised by his reply. 'I am here to spend time with you folk, and to encourage and persuade you that our beloved Pope and the Catholic Church is the correct and only one to follow.'

'Haw, haw, haw,' the men laughed, but they all wondered if once he was one of them because of his speech.

'Who else is coming up the mountains?' Father asked.

'No one, just me,' the monk replied.

Father could see he was harmless and nodded. 'I am sorry but you may have to stay for some time by the look of the weather.'

'Si.'

'Who are you? You speak with our tongue Are you a traitor? What's your name? Father demanded.

96

'My name is Peter Glosue, and I am from La Guardia, which is in the southern extremity of Italy. About forty years ago the papacy sent soldiers to villages in the southern area, to gather our youth. We were made to join and train as monks, or be killed. The papacy was short of church workers, also soldiers because of the wars that the Pope had instigated against foreign kings.'

'Si, that's fine but how do you know our tongue,' Father demanded.

The monk turned around to see if there was a seat in the room. He looked so tired.

Father noticed and had compassion for the old man. 'Si, please sit,' he said in a quiet voice.

Old Antonio came in with a warm jug of milk and several mugs, on a wooden tray. All present now sat with their mug in hand, quietly almost reverently waiting for the old monk to tell his tale.

'ONE DAY A LONG TIME ago, in the year 1340, two Waldense youths from your valleys sat in an inn in Torino. They spoke together of their somewhat sterile mountains and how hard it was to cultivate their small valleys. A stranger was listening to their discourse unnoticed by them.'

'Come with me and I will give you fertile fields,' the stranger invited.

The men, listening to the old monk started to mutter and whisper amongst themselves.

'Si, I was told about this, one said.

'He is correct,' another said.'

'Sh, sh, let him continue with his story,' Father suggested.

The monk continued, 'The boys went back to their

parents and talked over the conversation they had with the stranger, and the hopes he held out for them if they migrated to the southern land. They sent Vaudois explorers to the region, and they came back with a flattering report. Many families from these valleys migrated to the south of Italy and built the town, of La Guardia, where I am from. Si, I am one of your ancient brethren, but over the last century we lost our original faith.'

The Vaudois men became secretly excited. Here was their chance to bring a lost soul back to their fold. Maybe when he heard the wonderful hope, they all held in Jesus, he would share it with others on his travels.

MARIA SAT BY THE fire knitting. She used large wooden needles that her father had fashioned for her. 'Judith, do you like my knitting? Each square is a different colour. Mamma has placed lots of coloured balls in this basket for me to use. I am knitting your little one a nice rug.'

'Si, it is lovely dear,' answered Judith, who was thinking as she weaved how warm the house was.

It's amazing how these homes keep so cosy in winter. Our home in Pinerolo was built the same way; built with stones without mortar and the roof was made from large slabs of slate that Papa carved out of the mountains in flat, thin, squares. I watched Papa and my brothers build our home in such a way. There weren't any gaps to let in the cold,' she thought as she worked.

Father had returned and they could hear him talking with mother down in the barn.

'It was just a harmless old monk on a mission to convert us,' he explained as he carved the legs on Judith's baby's cradle.

Mother sat on a stool, milking the cow. As the milk squirted into her bucket she listened to father's story.

'Well, isn't Marco going to have lots of fun,' she laughed.

MARCO STOOD AND STRETCHED. He and Peter the monk, had been studying scriptures for two weeks. Old Antonio listened, while he quietly rocked in his chair by the fire. On the table in front of them was old Antonio's handwritten Bible. Marco walked to the fire and warmed his hands.

Peter stroked the leather cover of the Bible and wistfully spoke. 'I'm amazed that you have such a treasure in your hands. Do you realize that we only saw the Bible in church? It was never used to teach or train us. They only used the catechism for instruction. We were sent out on the road after three months of minimal training. They said we would learn on the way.'

Old Antonio rocking and smiling asked. 'Did you learn on the way?'

'Si, but not what I should have. I have learned that most folk out there are uneducated and full of superstition. If you tell them anything different from church teachings, you are a witch. Because of my upbringing, I also believed the same and encouraged this line of thinking in the community.'

Marco gently reminded the monk. 'Signor Glosue, remember what we read in Revelation chapter 14:12.' Marco recited the passage to him. Here is the patience of the saints; here are those who keep the commandments of God and the faith of Jesus. In the Bible God's book tells us clearly, that we must keep all the Ten Commandments, and also have the faith in Jesus. Jesus had great faith in his Father and we too must have this great faith. We must follow God's word as written in the Bible and not man's words or traditions. Signor Glosue, this is why we believe it's our duty to be itinerant missionaries. So, we can tell those poor deceived souls the truth. We must show them that their sins are forgiven at the cross.'

Peter sat staring at the cover of the Bible, not saying a word. A knock was heard on the door.

Signora entered with David Queyrus; Marco's relief guard.

'Here's your snow shoes Marco, I picked them up when I passed your place. You will need them as it's been snowing heavily for some time,' he said as he handed the shoes over.

Marco called out as he strapped his snow shoes on. 'Arrivèderci Signor Glosue, may God be with you?'

'Arrivèderci my young preacher and Grazie,' Peter replied in a soft muffled voice, as he hurriedly wiped tears from his old tired face with his ragged sleeve.

CHAPTER 16

SCHOOL OF BARBS

Marco trudged into the tiny courtyard of his family's home. His father was busy shovelling snow from the cobbled yard.

'Well look who's returned home,' father grinned, as he straightened and stretched.

Mother called out from the stables. 'Is Marco home Papa?'

Judith came from the winter storage room with her arms full of food for supper. 'How did it go Marco?

Maria hung over the balcony. 'It's Marco, Marco is home.' She ran down and jumped into his arms knocking him over and tumbling on top of him. She hugged him laughing. 'Scusare Marco, but I did miss you.'

'Let's go upstairs,' said mother, sticking her head out of the stables holding a bucket full of milk. 'We can all talk over supper.

JUDITH LAID IN HER warm bed looking out the window. It had stopped snowing and she could now see the full moon moving between the shadows of the night.

'I wonder how Pietro is going. I must write to him tomorrow,' she thought.

'Judith', Maria whispered 'Are you still awake?'

'Si.'

'Your little one, just kicked me in the back,' she giggled. 'If it's a girl, can we call her Ruth? If it's a boy, well I don't know.'

'Go to sleep and we will talk about it in the morning.'

MARCO TRUDGED UP THE steep mountain track to the 'School of the Barbs'. He was to stay there for winter with ten other youths, learning the ways of missionary colporteurs. While there he would experience hardship and deprivation, which would ready him for the work ahead. As he slowly moved forward, the lofty mountain peaks surrounded him in their robes of ice and snow.

Soon he came to a small hut. He knocked on the door. 'Signora it's Marco, can I come in?'

'Si.'

When he entered, he noticed at one end, were two noble-looking cows in a stable. At the other end, on a plank floor about six feet square, stood a bed, two stools, and a table, with a few dishes. This was Signora's winter quarters.

'Scusare Signora, I have parcels of food for you from Papa and Mamma.'

'What's your name?'

'Marco. My family are the de Vaux's from the village of Borgata Cyrus.

'Si, Grazie, I have something for you to take to the school.' She handed him two large blocks of cheese.

'Grazie, Signora.'

Marco continued up the track with his large, extremely heavy, basket on his back. 'I am so glad I am used to carrying heavy loads for Papa. Anyway, it will be worth it when I get there.'

Marco soon arrived at the 'School of the Barbs.' It stood high on a mountain ridge, hidden by the forest. It was a stone building typical of the area. To enter each of the three rooms the students would access them from the open verandah. There was a wood storage room underneath at one end.

The boys and the provisions had arrived and so had the freezing winter.

'We will be confined to our mountain quarters for three months,' Marco thought.

Soon it was Marco's turn to keep the fires burning in each room. He stepped out onto the open verandah and pulled his coat collar high above his ears. Homesickness swept over him.

'I wonder how the family is going. Old Peter the monk, at least will be a bit fatter and healthier by the time the snow melts. It would be so nice to have some of Mamma's cooking. I mustn't be such a baby as I will be going soon into the mission fields, like Pietro. I

wonder what he's doing. I believe the weather is much milder in Firenze. I would love to see his hospital.' His thoughts raced, as he looked across the snow-covered wilderness with icicles hanging from the branches of large oaks. Icy mountain peaks surrounded and towered above them, hiding the college in their bosoms. All was white and frozen. Marco hurried to the storage room and quickly with his large basket carried wood to the enclosed boxes, sitting at each door. He had to move quickly or he would freeze.

When he came back inside, he removed his coat and hung it on a hook by the door for the next boy. The Barb was speaking to the class. 'We have studied scripture in our morning classes. This you all excelled in. You have been well taught by your parents since early childhood. Now we will discuss this afternoon, ways to present these truths to the uneducated and the wealthy. I must mention that translating the Bible passages from French to Romano is going along nicely. Marco, France, and Jean your careful script-writing of the 'New Testament has been very time-consuming, taking you into the night, but the project is worthy of your dedication. Now, remember, we are testing you on your oral Latin and Romano tongue before the term is over. You are dismissed for dinner,' he said.

After dinner, Marco, France, and Jean worked together, washing and drying the dishes.

'Did you know they have opened the old Catholic Church and a convent in Torre Pellice?' France explained.

'No, that can't be right. They wouldn't dare. This is our valley and town. The folk wouldn't let them,' Jean replied.

Marco listened and explained, 'Si, it's correct. They have opened the buildings. Old Peter, the monk with whom I was

104

studying, told me about it. They hope the monks will have lots of converts.'

'Well, they're wrong. The buildings will be empty. No one will attend, just wait and see,' Jean said.

'Si, Si, that's right,' they all agreed.

Many weeks later Marco grabbed his coat and headed to the door. It was again his turn to fetch wood for the fires. When on the verandah, he hurriedly pulled his coat collar above his ears. Looking up he noticed that the icicles hanging from the trees had melted, and leaves were forming on the branches. The brook was now a cascading torrent and could be heard thundering over the precipice.

'It's spring,' Marco shouted. 'Spring, is here,' he said as he bounded into the dining room.

Two weeks later all the boys were packed and ready to go home. Wearing his father's snow shoes, Marco trudged down the mountain track towards his village, and home.

CHAPTER 17

FIRENZE HOSPITAL

*P*ietro walked through the 'Mercy of Firenze Hospital,' and passed through the women's ward with its long rows of beds, and its nurses' station in the centre. Nodding to his staff, he walked out into the foyer and passed the cloister. Behind the light-filtered window, there was a sculpture of the Virgin and child accompanied by statues of two small angels. Stepping outside he walked down the narrow laneway, past the monastery, which was now the men's section, and then walked to the hospital garden, where medicinal plants were grown for the hospital pharmacy. He sat on a bench under a large bare oak, that was budding new leaves. A rush of concern washed over him as he opened Judith's letter.

'I hope she's well,' he thought.

'Dear Pietro,
It has been a long cold winter. It has been snowing most days and we have been passing the time with practical occupations. Mamma has been busy with daily chores, and feeding and caring for all of us. Marco is away at the 'School of the Barbs. Spring is on the way, and the snow is melting. The little one is due soon, and I am going to call her Ruth

if it's a girl or Paul if it's a boy. We have been making clothes for summer and the little one. You should see the lovely rocking chair papa has made for me. I miss you terribly.'

Judith.

Students' happy chatter as they walked by, made Pietro look up, and he realized he was late for his morning lecture.

'Today is anatomy and they have a fresh cadaver to study,' he thought as he walked to class. *'As chief of staff and the hospital's only surgeon, it's my duty to train these young Signors in the hospital school to become physicians, surgeons, or pharmacists. Lord, please help me to have the ability to teach, and the skill to demonstrate,'* he prayed.

As he entered the classroom, he noticed ten students standing around the cadaver, ready for his lecture.

'Buongiorno class.'

'Buongiorno Signor,' they responded.

'Are you all here?'

'We are all here, Signor.

'Let's start then.' Pietro cut into the leg and after cutting for some time, he exposed the muscles.

'Can you name the muscles I just exposed?' Pietro asked. He pointed to the muscle which flexed the knee.

'Signor, is it the gastrocnemius?' a student asked.

'Signor, it's popliteal,' another answered.

A new student, who had his head down sketching, spoke. 'Signor, can I show you, my sketches? It will make it easier.'

Pietro nodded, 'Si, you're new here. What's your name?'

'My name is Leonardo da Vinci and I was sent by the art Academy.'

'Well, an art student, that's interesting. I wonder what he has drawn,' Pietro thought.

The student stepped forward, holding a large sketchbook. He held up his sketches and they were the most detailed and correct anatomy sketches that Pietro had ever seen. 'See,' the student said, as he pointed to the gastrocnemius muscle; 'it gives flexion to the leg, and he pointed to another muscle, 'and the knee flexion is aided by the popliteal muscle which rotates the tibia.'

'Well done,' Pietro answered impressed. 'Can I have a closer look at your sketches after class?

'Si Signor,' Leonardo answered with a nod of his head, and he walked back to his position around the cadaver.

After class, the student stayed back and explained why he was attending the surgical classes.

'I'm an art student at the 'Academy of the Medici' and my early mentor and great friend Verrocchio, made arrangements for me to attend your classes. He felt if I had a thorough understanding of the human form it would help me with my paintings.'

Pietro thought to himself as he walked back to his quarters. *'I have heard of this artist and I believe his work is so outstanding that when he was only fourteen years old and studying under Verrocchio, he painted on his mentor's canvas an angel. In every way, his work was better than Verrocchio's. It embarrassed his teacher so much that he gave up instructing students. I believe they are still friends and Verrocchio advises Leonardo in his pursuit of art.'*

When he was back at his quarters Pietro washed and was dressing to meet Lorenzo in the palace's drawing room, when there was a knock at his door. His servant opened the door to Lorenzo's wife's maid.

'Si, Signor de Vaux is in,' answered Pietro's servant. 'Please wait until I have delivered the letter to him.' The letter read:

Dear Pietro,

I wish to invite you to dinner at 8 pm and before dinner, I wish you to discreetly meet me in my quarters to examine my scalp. I am having skin problems.

Pietro quickly wrote his note of acceptance for dinner and his medical appointment. He went downstairs to the foyer and personally placed it in the hands of Duchess Clarice's maid.

He stared intently at the maid's hair and thought, *'By what I can see, she doesn't seem to have her mistress's skin problems.*

The maid looked at him worried and scurried away.

PIETRO STRODE QUICKLY down the street to the palace. It was still early and the sun was high above the buildings. The guards at the main gate nodded and let him through without question. The ground floor was a defended courtyard surrounded by guard rooms and quarters for men at arms. He climbed the outside staircase passing the upper floors, which were the household proper, and then onto the roof.

Signoras of the household were sitting on the rooftop in the sun with their hair flowing out around large circular disks, which they wore like hats, in an attempt to bleach their hair. To add to this, was the urine, that they combed through their hair to improve the bleaching process. The atmosphere stunk like bambinos in dirty swaddling clothes. Pietro quickly left before he was noticed. He now had the proof he needed to present to the Duchess.

Back in the main lobby, Pietro was escorted to Lorenzo's study. When he entered the room Lorenzo was standing with a tall young fellow, examining detailed sketches. Both swung around.

Lorenzo extended his hand. 'Pietro I'm glad you are here. Have you met Leonardo, our resident artist?'

'Si, this morning in my anatomy class,' Pietro responded with a laugh.

'That's good,' nodded Lorenzo, and turned back to the charts. 'Just look at these sketches, have you seen anything like it?' he asked and then continued. 'These are prints Leonardo has drawn of murals he's going to paint on the walls of our government buildings. Would you like beautiful artwork like these on your hospital walls?'

'Grazie Lorenzo, but for now good anatomy charts for the classroom would be more beneficial.' Pietro replied.

'Consider it done,' Lorenzo laughed.

Several servants entered the room with trays of food and hot drinks. The men continued to talk at length about plans to beautify Firenze. They discussed covering the walls of government buildings with beautiful art, and then it was designing beautiful parks and gardens. Leonardo's knowledge as a botanist would help to achieve this. Next, they talked about the hospital's medical services, and the medicinal gardens. This time it was Pietro's turn to show his medical and herbal knowledge and to express his needs and concerns in his field of work.

Lorenzo looked around and realized it was getting late. 'We are going to my bank. Would you like to come along Pietro? I have someone I would like you to meet.'

Soon they were travelling along the cobbled street. City residents walked along the narrow street, which the coach was slowly traversing. When at the Medici Bank, the driver stayed with the coach and horses while they entered through the backdoor, away from the eyes of the clients.

'I would like you, Pietro, to meet my friend and bank manager Jacob Isaac,' introduced Duke Lorenzo. No one needed to tell Pietro that the manager was a Jew. His clothes, features, and of course his name all pointed to his identity.

Signor Isaac nodded with indifference to Pietro and then turned to Leonardo. 'We have been using your double ledger system and it's brilliant. It makes it so easy to track the comings and goings of this bank's business. Could you come into my office, I need more help with these books?' He tapped with his fingers, the books in his arms.

'So, Leonardo the artist is also a mathematician and a botanist. What's next? I have been told he's brilliant,' Pietro thought.

'Let's go back to the palace and leave the banking business to the experts,' suggested Duke Lorenzo.

As the coach driver struggled to negotiate his way through the crowd, the duke watched Pietro closely. He cleared his throat and spoke. 'Pietro you and Signor Isaac have a lot in common as you are both Jewish type people. He is wise in the ways of the world and can teach you your place here in Firenze. He then changed his attitude when he thought Pietro didn't understand what he was hinting about. His face hardened and he looked quite angry. 'Pietro there are two things you must remember never to do. One is to correct the Pope, and the other is to criticise my government. If you remember this you will keep your head.'

He stared hard at Pietro, who pushed himself back into the padded seat. Pietro wished the seat would close in and around him.

'Si,' Pietro nodded and lowered his head.

'I wonder if someone has reported our Bible classes. Pietro thought. *We have been very discreet when we share the scriptures. For the Duke to class us the same as Jews, he knows better than that. We keep the Bible Sabbath but aren't Jews. They don't believe in Jesus and His resurrection. He is just warning me to be silent about my faith. I must warn the others.'*

The duke leaned out of the carriage window and waved to his citizens. 'It's a good thing our city isn't anti-Semite isn't it,' he said looking back at Pietro with a smile. 'I believe you have to discuss a medical problem with my wife, so let's go straight there. We can't keep the royal signora waiting can we,' he now chuckled and the other subject seemed to be forgotten, but Pietro knew better.

DUKE LORENZO STOOD next to Pietro as he examined his wife's head. Pietro cleared his throat and thought before he spoke. 'Duchess you've burnt your skin, and it will take some time to heal. If you massage this herbal formula I have here, through your hair it will heal your burnt scalp and kill the infection that has set in.'

'Si,' Lorenzo said. 'Go on, tell her what she and her friends must stop doing.'

'Lorenzo,' she squealed. 'Please don't embarrass me.'

Her maid busied herself clearing the dressing table; her face becoming a darker shade of red by the moment. She kept looking at Lorenzo, who noticed, and looked her up and down several times.

'Is that a baby bump I can see under her full skirt?' Pietro thought.

Duke Lorenzo turned back to his wife. 'You embarrass yourself Clarice my dear,' he answered grim-faced. 'Tell her Pietro.'

Pietro once again cleared his throat. 'I think if you use lemon juice or vinegar to bleach your hair it will be more beneficial. I have bottles here for you, and I have written the formula for both, on the labels.'

Duke Lorenzo laughed, 'I think I will make you a politician. What tact! Now don't forget dinner is at eight,' he said looking Pietro up and down.

'Si, Grazie, I will be here in time, and dressed appropriately,' Pietro answered with a slight bow, grinning.

Pietro arrived just in time. The guests were entering the family's dining room. He was dressed in Signora Ricciardi's husband's formal brown suit and cloak.

'I hope I have now dressed appropriately,' he thought.

'Signor de Vaux,' announced the Butler as he took Pietro's cloak.

Pietro followed a waiter to his chair. The large table was set with fine white China bearing the Medici family crest around the edge. The crystal glasses, jugs, and vases with fresh flowers were the finest in the world, made in Firenze's local shops. Crystal chandeliers hung low over the table making everything sparkle. Pietro looked at the feminists who had been sunning themselves earlier in the day. They sat eating, smiling, and talking. They were dressed in beautiful ornate silk gowns, with their bleached hair held above their heads with golden nets.

Pietro smiled to himself, and thought, *'If I told them that I knew their secret I wonder how quickly their smiling faces would turn to horror. I hope Duchess Clarice advises them, on another way of bleaching'*.

After dinner, they went into the drawing room. The walls were covered in wonderful murals, painted by Leonardo da Vinci, who walked with Duke Lorenzo's guests, slowly explaining the stories depicted.

Soon they all settled in comfortable chairs and to their surprise, they were to be entertained by their host the duke himself. He sat at his harpsichord and sang and played melodies that he had composed, and everyone was enthralled with his great musical talents.

CHAPTER 18

POPE'S VISIT

Several weeks later, Pietro attended the Duchess in her private rooms. 'Signora, your head isn't so inflamed. I hope you have advised your friends on a better way of bleaching,' he said as he packed his medical case.

'Mamma, Mamma,' the Medici children called, as they rushed into her room, not waiting to be announced properly.

'Children, children,' laughed the Duchess as she hugged the boys, who had just returned home from boarding school.

'Mamma you must hear my stories first,' Maddalena laughed, pushing and nudging with her elbows, her brothers away from her mother 'I have so much to tell you about Signora Palmisano and her wonderful teachings on humanism. We must talk also about my gown for the ball. Mamma, we have little time to shop for it.' *She looked around at her brothers and thought perhaps they should first tell their stories, after all; she had serious business to discuss.* 'Mamma, the boys can go first,' she said and stood next to her mother, holding her hand.

The Duchess looked around at the boys. *'Dear me they look so thin and pale. I must speak to Lorenzo about them,'* She thought.

Her maid came in. 'Come children let your Mamma rest. You can talk to her later.'

'It's alright Gina; I want to hear their stories. She then spoke to her son. 'Giovanni, could you please escort Doctor de Vaux down to Papa's office? I believe he has business to discuss with Papa.'

As they walked slowly down the stairs they chatted. 'Tell me what you are learning at school Giovanni? Pietro asked, interested in the lives of these royal children.

'Well, it's not like here. The food is awful, with stale bread and potatoes mostly. They said we will need to become tough if we expect to lead men in war. Who wants to do that? They whip us if we don't obey them, and the hours are so long.

'What do you learn,' Pietro asked, changing the subject.

We learn Latin, Greek logic, and philosophy. Also, we are taught the ways of a warrior and courtier which includes riding, swordsmanship, dancing, and of course the art of war.

Pietro was impressed. 'What about learning to become a banker and statesman, like your father,' he asked.

'No, they are our family's secrets and Papa will teach me when I am part of the family's business.'

'Well perhaps how to become a good cardinal if you are part of the papal business,' Pietro responded.

'I think that's it,' Giovanni laughed. 'They are sending me to Rome to the 'Cardinal School of Learning. I hope it will be better there.'

'You will become a little Samuel,' Pietro teased.

Giovanni frowned.

Pietro thought, *He doesn't know the Bible story of the little boy who became a priest, but what do you expect, most people even the educated, haven't been taught the Bible.'*

Walking down the stairs they met Duke Lorenzo and Gerardo coming from the office.

'I must go straight to the bank, as an urgent business has

just developed,' Lorenzo explained. He ruffled his son's hair, as they walked off, with Giovanni happily chatting with him about school.

GERARDO PLACED AN ARM around Pietro's shoulder. 'Well, I'm glad I have you to myself, as I need your help in choosing an engagement ring for Teodorina. I am supposed to present the ring at the ball after the speeches, but you know me I can't wait that long.'

Pietro was shocked. 'Gerardo you are asking the wrong person. Our people are very simple and jewellery isn't something we indulge in.'

'Si, that's why you are going to help me because our people wear far too much, and all at the same time; Teodorina has spent most of her life in the Vatican Convent. She was planning on becoming a nun until I came along. Her taste is simple and mine has been spoilt by the lifestyle I have become accustomed to, so my dear friend I need you to balance my over-indulged taste.'

They walked down the Uffizi thoroughfare while they talked, and soon were on the Vecchio Bridge. Gerardo passed the gold shops, lining the walkway, and came to a small shop tucked in a corner, near the centre of the bridge. This is my friend Benevento's shop. He doesn't mind us calling him Ben. He has placed several rings aside for me to consider.

Ben looked up as they entered the shop. 'Buongiorno Gerardo, I can see you are ready to make a decision.'

'Si Ben, let me introduce you to my friend and Firenze's new hospital director, Pietro de Vaux.'

Ben knew as soon as he looked at Pietro by his height and

117

vitality that he was from the mountains, and his name de Vaux was Waldensian. He didn't let on that he knew, and turned and busied himself with the tray of rings. He turned back and placed them before the youth. They were breathtakingly huge and very ornate with many different styles and coloured jewels.

'Well, what do you think Pietro? You must help me,' Gerardo pleaded.

In the corner of the tray, a ring caught Pietro's eye and he went to pick it up.

Ben spoke, 'No, surely not that ring when there are so many larger more impressive rings to choose from. What about this one?' He said, as he picked up a ring with a huge ruby in the shape of a flower and large diamonds two rows deep covering a wide band.

Pietro continued to pick up the ring that caught his eye. It was on a plain gold band, and set high in the middle was a large sparkling solitaire diamond, that was beautiful in its simplicity.

'Si that's the one,' Gerardo agreed. 'It's simple but magnificent. It's perfect in size and cut. Grazie Pietro, I know Teodorina will love it.'

SEVERAL WEEKS LATER the Pope's party arrived at the palace and participated in the official visitation of the city. While at the Cathedral, the Pope and his two children joined Lorenzo's family and attended High Mass. On leaving the building the Pope smiled benignly at the people gathered outside and gently murmured. 'Bless you, my children,' as they knelt and kissed his hands or the hem of his robes. His plump white hand, sparkling with gems, touched a baby's cheeks as he passed. 'Bless you little one.'

Their official party walked past the people crowding the streets.

Lorenzo walked with the official party, introducing them to the wonderful work that Leonardo da Vinci, had accomplished in the government buildings. The murals were magnificent.

'Please send him to Rome. We would like murals on our buildings as well,' the Pope said enviously.

'Si, Your Holiness. He can go back with you after the ball,' the duke answered.

Next, they visited the City Hall, where a pantomime was to take place. The seating was specially positioned to view the magnificent murals covering the walls. The pantomime started and accomplished artists acted in plays on current events. Later clowns appeared which the children especially enjoyed. Later they went back to the palace and their rooms to rest and prepare for the ball that evening.

CHAPTER 19

THE GRAND BALL

Pietro entered the palace's great hall. It was past midnight and the ball had been in progress for some time. The scene before him took his breath away. Massive sparkling chandeliers hung low from the high ceiling, reflecting the many lit candles sitting within the crystals. Most glorious murals covered the walls. Tall elegant glass doors with red velvet drapes led out to the rooftop garden.

Men in velvet jackets and matching breeches with white knitted hoses danced with signoras in shimmering silk gowns. They wore their hair high, held in place with finely crafted exquisite tiaras, encrusted with sparkling jewels. Around their necks and on their ears were matching jewels. Servants moved amongst the guests carrying large trays with crystal goblets filled with the best Tuscan wine from the duke's vineyards.

Pietro stood and watched the signoras in their beautiful gowns, dancing and whirling in time with the glorious music. He felt a tap on his shoulder and turned to see Enzo and Carlo dressed in bright velvet evening attire, nervously grinning at him.

'Have you been here long?'

'Si, but we have kept in the shadows,' Enzo quivered.

'Can you see Gerardo?' Pietro asked his friends.

'Si, over there,' Enzo pointed.

Gerardo was dancing with a beautiful young girl with long dark hair flowing down her back that was held in place with a simple pearl tiara. She wore a white gown, with its sleeves and hem encrusted in pearls. The couple danced, mesmerized by each other, gently whispering and smiling together.

The Pope watched with interest and wiped his brow with a perfumed handkerchief.

Now his son Franceschetti danced with Lorenzo's daughter Maddalena. She wore a crystal blue silk dress and her fair hair was held back by a fine gold net. As she danced, she stood stiff and proud. Franceschetti hardly noticed her. His head continually turned to look at others. They both knew they were to become a match of convenience for their parents.

The Pope shrewdly watched the young couple and thought, *'Young Signorina with your high and mighty Humanistic ideas, my son Franceschetti will marry you and this will greatly increase my wealth, and in return, your thirteen-year-old brother Giovanni will obtain the cardinal hat, and by the look of you two it will only be a marriage of convenience not love.'*

Gerardo and Teodorina whirled around the floor stopping in front of Pietro and his friends.

Gerardo spoke to his fiancée. 'Teodorina these are my friends I have been telling you about,' and before anyone could say anymore, he continued, 'Pietro I have been waiting for you. I told them not to make any announcements until I've indicated.'

Pietro noticed the ring on Teodorina's hand and grinned and nodded. He looked up to see the Pope, in a red silk cloak and white tunic sitting on the other side of the hall. He was staring at them. Gerardo and Teodorina danced and whirled away into the throng on the floor, in time with the music that vibrated through the hall. Gerardo mischievously grinned over Teodorina's shoulder giving his friends a big wink, as they danced towards the Pope's party.

Carlo responded in a fearful whisper. 'The man who is responsible for the slaughter of our people is in this very hall, and right now is staring at us.'

'Si, he is Pietro,' Enzo squeaked.

Both Carlo and Enzo shrunk back into the shadows while Pietro fearfully continued to watch the events taking place, silently sweating and shaking.

Duke Lorenzo leaned over and spoke to the Pope. The Pope nodded, still staring at Pietro. When Gerardo and Teodorina approached the Pope, the official party stood. Duke Lorenzo held his hand high in the air. The orchestra immediately stopped playing and the dancers quickly left the floor. Then the official party walked to the stage. Teodorina stood next to her father the Pope with Gerardo at her side. Duke Lorenzo stood a little further behind. The people stood, and all were silent.

Pope Innocent started his speech. 'Wonderful citizens of Firenze, the most advanced and wealthy city in the world, I wish to remind you that you are also subjects of God's worldwide Roman Catholic Church, which is the true and perfect representative of God's church on earth. Our ordained leaders have God's authority to interpret the Bible, His Holy Word, and you must do as we say.' He looked straight at Pietro as if he knew who he was. Now Pietro felt terrified. The Pope continued. 'Today we have been part of your wonderful festival and now this evening the grand ball is held in honour of the betrothal of my daughter Teodorina and the Duke's nephew Gerardo.

Could you please fill your glasses for a toast?' There was a scurry of movement with servants and guests filling their glasses.

Duke Lorenzo and the Pope held their glasses in the air. The people quickly followed.

The duke in a loud voice called, 'Teodorina and Gerardo.'

The people answered, 'Teodorina and Gerardo,' and they all drank.

As soon as the toast was given Lorenzo went back to his seat, but the Pope was still walking to his when clowns and court Jesters bounced onto the floor. Lorenzo sat amused with the pantomime. The people cheered and clapped.

The Pope was angry with the lack of respect towards him and his papal position, and he fumed to himself as he sat there. '*How dare they! The humanistic ways of this city are breeding disrespect for the papacy and my God-given deity. I must bring Lorenzo and his people to their knees.*'

Carlo and Enzo were petrified. As they stepped out from the shadows, to nudge Pietro to leave, they noticed the Pope was staring or was it snarling at them.

The Pope thought to himself as he watched them, pale and anxious. '*I am sure those signors employed by Lorenzo are Waldensians; they must be exterminated, but my hands are tied while they are under Lorenzo's employ. It amazes me how the mountain folk are so tall and strong with such well-formed features. I am told they can read and are highly educated in religious matters. Well, they must remember that only I, the Pope, and my cardinals whom I choose, have the right to interpret the Bible, and it's treason if anybody tries that isn't appointed by me.*

123

CHAPTER 20

ORPHANAGE

*C*arlo left the ball and rushed to the hospital. He twisted the corner of his moustache and thought, *'I will go straight to the maternity ward. Many babies are born in the early hours of the morning. As supervisor of this ward, the poor attending the hospital may need my advice.'*

After visiting his patients with their new babies, he left and walked quickly down the street. Turning the corner, he walked next to the 'Innocent's Orphanage' building. It was late and dark. A cold breeze stroked his face.

Is that a person I can see walking in the shadows of the orphanage wall? He thought.

A candle in the street lantern threw a dim light on a recess in the wall. *There they are at the recess and they're pulling the cord.* The recess swung around and was replaced by a receptacle with a basket.

Si, they are placing a baby into the basket and they're now pulling the cord, and si, the receptacle is turning. It has taken the infant inside leaving an empty recess outside, I was told about this receptacle. Just look at that, with their head down they hurry away.

The person in the shadows didn't notice Carlo watching. *I can't see if it is a servant on an errand for their mistress or a poor peasant girl. I must go in and see if there are any clues to the baby's identity,* he thought.

He knocked on the large front door and a nun with a lamp arrived.

'Can I help you?'

'Si, may I take a look at the baby you just received in the orphanage's receptacle basket?'

'Signor, that isn't allowed.'

A senior nun passed the entrance. She stopped and listened. She realized immediately who Carlo was. 'Sister Florien I will take care of the matter, please continue with your duties,' she said kindly.

'Grazie Sister Susanna,' replied the other, and hurried away.

'Please come this way, Signor.' She led him down the passage and into the outside room with the receptacle. The baby was asleep in the basket.

'Can I examine the infant,' Carlo requested.

'Si.'

He carefully placed the baby on a table and undid its swaddling clothes. It was a boy. The outer cloth was made of fine wool and the inner white linen, with the Medici crest stamped in the corner. Carlo looked up, shocked.

'Please Sister gives me the bambino's swaddling clothes, and not a word to anybody. Take the infant to the nursery and keep him there until I tell you otherwise.'

She did as she was told, handing Carlo the swaddling clothes and quickly dressing the infant in the orphanage apparel.

'I will let myself out Sister,' Carlo said, 'and not a word now.'

'Si,' she said and quietly left the room.

'Grazie Sister,' he softly called after her, as he unlatched the door.

THE NEXT MORNING Carlo hurried to the barber shop with its striped red and white poles. 'I wonder if Enzo is here.'

Nodding to the barber, who was cutting a rotund signor's beard, Carlo walked through the shop to the clinic room at the back. Here he found Enzo with a student. They were about to bleed a man lying on the table. Enzo was explaining where to cut when he looked up.

'Carlo, how good to see you,' Enzo said swinging his arm while holding the knife. All jumped back. 'Scusare,' he said embarrassed, putting the knife down.

'One day you will do some real damage talking with your hands,' Carlo smirked. 'Do you know where I can find Pietro? He's not in the hospital wards, or at home.'

'No sorry.'

Carlo then went into the dispensary next door. Here he found Leonardo da Vinci with the chemist, working out formulas. He was writing notes, next to plants he had sketched in his botanist notebook.

'Buongiorno, Leonardo have you seen Pietro this morning?'

'Si, he's in the hospital's lecture room marking papers.'

'Grazie.'

Carlo realized it was late and hurried to the maternity ward. *I'll catch Pietro later and discuss what we need to do with the abandoned infant,* He thought.

SEVERAL DAYS LATER Pietro sat quietly in the lecture room, correcting papers. He kept an eye on the palace gates, and there it was the Pope's carriage. 'Good the Pope and his family are returning to Rome, and the cavalry is leading the procession.' He watched the captain call instructions, as they moved forward and traversed the congested street.

Breathing a sigh of relief he thought, *'At long last, I can go and see Gerardo. I wish to discuss with him my fears about attending his wedding in Rome.'*

With a quick prayer for the right words, he rushed to the palace and met Gerardo in the courtyard mounting his horse.

'Gerardo,' he called. I was hoping to talk to you on the matter of attending your wedding.'

'Don't worry my friend; I know how dangerous it will be. I will talk to Lorenzo when I get back and beg him to write to the Pope, for security and safety for you, while you're in Rome. I will ask Lorenzo to explain to the Pope your important position, here at the hospital. I am now going on an errand for Duke Lorenzo and won't be back for at least two weeks. Arrivèderci,' he said, waving as he cantered out the palace gates.

PIETRO SAT IN HIS lecture room, quiet and pensive. 'It has been two weeks since the ball, and Gerardo's departure. I wonder when he will get back.' He continued writing his letter to Judith when suddenly Carlo burst into his room.

'Pietro, I need to talk to you.'

Pietro indicated for his friend to sit.

Carlo twiddled with his moustache quieting himself; took a deep breath and started again. 'The night of the ball I went back to the hospital, and on the way home I walked passed the orphanage and saw a small baby being placed in the basket. I went in and found the bambino wrapped in Medici swaddling clothes. Pietro, I need you to go to Lorenzo and ask him to check with his servants, to see which maid delivered an infant. I should have come to you earlier, but I thought if we reported the birth in some way, it would get us in trouble. But not reporting it has also worried me because the signora may need medical help.

Pietro looked out the window and sat thinking. 'The Duchess's maid looked very pregnant, I wonder if it was her, and the duke noticed her as well. I wonder if I should go to him.'

Pietro turned around, 'Si, I will go there straight away. It's only early evening, and a good time to approach the duke as he should be home from his 'Medici Bank.'

They walked to the palace gates. It was a mild evening, with blossoms falling from the trees. Pietro noticed, and spoke of Judith. 'I was just reading a letter from Judith and she said the snow is melting and spring has arrived in the mountains. She has only a short while before her baby is born. I wonder what it will be.' They chatted and then parted.

Pietro knocked on the hallway's large front door. 'Come this way.' The butler escorted Pietro to Lorenzo's office in the upper chambers.

'Doctor de Vaux please wait here,' he said and indicated a chair in the hallway. 'The duke is busy at the moment, conducting business with others, in his office.'

Pietro sat there contemplating what he was going to say when the duke started yelling.

'The Pope did what? He yelled, and his shoes clicked on the floor as he paced back and forth.

'He has threatened to take the Duke of Milano's investiture from him and to leave him without shares in taxes and indulgences. Also, to increase the tariffs set out for nobles if he didn't rescind the agreement with you,' answered the other voice.

Gerardo is back; I wonder what went wrong, Pietro thought.

'Who informed on us? How did the Pope get to know about our agreement with the duke?' Lorenzo screamed and clicking could be heard as he paced back and forth.

Gerardo mumbled something.

'And what did the duke do? With all the wars he's been participating in of late, he needs money to keep Milano afloat, so he must sell the town Imola and its surrounding land,' Lorenzo gruffly reasoned.

'Well, the Duke is a very shrewd businessman. When he couldn't sell Imola and the land to you for two thousand ducats, he decided to sell it instead, to the Pope for four thousand ducats. He's smart and knows who to bite,' he laughed.

Lorenzo stopped pacing and swung around. 'Jacob, I hope our bank didn't lend the Pope money when he was visiting with us,' he growled.

So, Jacob, the bank's manager is also present in the room, Pietro thought.

'No, but the Pope did go to our branch in Rome when he returned home.'

'What were they thinking of,' Lorenzo screamed.

But before he could go on, Jacob continued. 'Your Lordship, they refused him, so he went to our rival bankers, the Pazzis, and borrowed the money from them, and purchased the land and Imola.'

'Si, right from under my nose,' Lorenzo whispered in a furious hiss. 'The Pope has placed the Florentine Republic in a dire situation because we are now without a route to the sea to export our Alum.

Jacob thought for a moment and then spoke. 'I heard when the Pope takes over a city or province, he leaves the original rulers in place to continue with state business as usual. Who is the governor in Imola, Gerardo?'

Gerardo answered him. 'The son of the King of Naples is placed up there. He is also the Duke of Milano's nephew. There has been a controversy over who should pay his salary.'

'Well, there's our answer,' Jacob laughed. 'Duke Lorenzo, why don't you pay the King's son a large yearly salary, with an agreement from the King that you and your army can use the trade routes to the sea for your Alum mines? You will achieve the upper hand on the Pope without war. The Pope wouldn't dare fight the King of Naples as he resides close to Rome and is all-powerful.

'Bravo, Bravo,' Lorenzo cheered. 'I will send a letter and the money with my friend who is heading back to Rome. He will see that the King of Naples receives it safely,' he sat down to write his letter.

Pietro decided to leave quickly. '*I should have left earlier, as I will be in real trouble if they see me sitting here listening,*' he thought as he walked quickly away.

WHEN PIETRO ENTERED THE Duchess's room, he found her sitting at the dressing table with her maid brushing out her braids.

'Nice to see you, Pietro, please do come in,' Smiled Duchess Clarice, tilting her head, so she could look at him.

'Grazie,' responded Pietro, as he walked over to the

Duchess. Her maid stepped aside and he noticed that she was no longer pregnant.

'I must be very careful in what I say to the Duchess,' Pietro thought.

He lent over the Duchess and examined her hair. 'Your head is completely healed. That small area around the back of your ears has healed as well. I'm glad that you've carried out what I suggested.'

He then went to his medical bag and handed the Duchess swaddling clothes with the Medici monogram. She looked into the mirror at her maid who was standing back. Her eyes were dark, her lips tight and she shook her head ever so slightly at the maid. It was obvious she was furious with her and needed privacy to sort out the problem.

'Please scusare, I will go now,' Pietro mumbled, and he quickly left.

CHAPTER 21

JUDITH IN THE MOUNTAINS

Six year-old Maria looked over the balcony. 'Judith, Mamma said it's time to collect our cow, and I'm coming to take care of you. I will hold your hand so you won't fall,' she called.

'Grazie, si that will be nice Maria,' Judith laughed, as she watched Maria jump down the stairs one by one to the courtyard, where she stood waiting.

On their way to the mountain pastures, they passed cottages with their vines hanging over the walls full of ripening grapes. Their home gardens had been turned over and seeds planted. They passed Marco and father ploughing the field; preparing the soil for its summer crops. Marco looked up and waved.

As they passed the cliff face Judith pointed, 'Maria looks at those tiny mice.'

Maria smiled as she watched field mice eating small wild strawberries hidden amongst clumps of grass, which dotted the stony ridges. Maria nodded; 'Si, cheeky little things, aren't they?' she said and started to skip. She then looked up at Judith. 'Is my skipping worrying you? Why are you holding your stomach, Judith?'

Judith half bent over groaned. 'Perhaps we can walk along without holding hands, and then I can hold my baby in my stomach,' Judith suggested, flinching with pain.

'Should I go back Judith thought, *but I still have two weeks before my time and they say it's normal to get small pains before the baby comes? I will stand straight, and breathe deeply. That should make the pain go away.'*

She looked up at the lofty summits, which surrounded their little valley, with their snowcapped tips shimmering in the sun. *'I love it here. It's so peaceful and the family is so kind. Oh no, here it comes again.'* Judith groaned and doubled over clasping Maria's shoulder for balance.

'Get help, Maria,' Judith groaned in agony. Marco was watching and strode over to them.

'It's alright, here let me help you, Judith,' Marco said. Judith jumped as she didn't see or hear him approach.

'Judith, try and walk between the pains,' he suggested.

'Mamma, Mamma, Maria yelled. 'Judith can't walk.

Mother rushed down the stairs to help Judith. 'Careful Marco' let's get her up these stairs. If we place our shoulders under her armpits, we can half walk and half carry her,' mother suggested. 'It's time my dear. We must get ready as the little one is on the way. Maria, you go with Marco to

133

fetch the cow. Marco let Papa know what's happening on the way passed,' mother ordered.

Marco walked with Maria, as slowly as he could, to the far pastures and then back to their cottage.

They sat together in the barn for a long time. Marco milked and Maria fiddled.

'Marco when can I go up,' she pleaded.

'Not until we hear the baby cry,' he explained once again.

Suddenly a long, loud, excruciating wail came from the room above. Maria looked up terrified. Then the howling of a very young infant was heard.

'It's here,' shouted Maria as she rushed up the stairs. She burst into the room to see a little red and slimy creature being wrapped in Judith's swaddling clothes.

'The Bambina has arrived Maria,' Judith whispered. She laid back on the pillows exhausted, as mother de Vaux placed the little bundle into her arms.

'MARCO LET'S GO TO Torre Pellice's woods. The woodcutter said he needs help clearing the fallen branches caused by the winter storms. With such a cold winter, we are nearly out of wood, so let's help, and clear it for him. We can leave the signoras' home as they are occupied with the little Bambina at the moment,' Father said grinning, giving Marco a knowing wink.

When in the woods, they picked up branches that fitted into the cart. Suddenly a scream was heard.

'Stay close to me,' father instructed. He grabbed his axe and moved quietly in the direction from which it came.

Two papal dignitaries dressed in scarlet cloaks dragged four young children out of their hiding place beneath a wagon. Two nuns appeared and dragged the children toward the old broken-down walls of an ancient fort. Inside the walls, was a cave. The dignitaries in scarlet mounted their horses, which sensed the tension in their riders and began to snort and whinny and jump about. The dignitaries quickly rode away.

Suddenly a woman leapt up and ran across to the two soldiers near the wagon. In the Patois tongue, she screamed at them. 'You can't take our children. We are in our valleys. Who permitted you to come here? Wait until our folk hear what you're up to,' she screamed.

She was ferocious, biting and scratching and kicking out with her bare feet. One of the soldiers silenced her with his fist and hauled her by the hair to a swelling group of women and their children who were tied by their hands to the wagon.

Marco whispered to his father who conceded with a grunt of annoyance.

Marco ran towards them, scattering pecking chickens from the woodcutter's nearby farm.

'After him,' the soldier by the wagon ordered. Marco turned and sprinted in the direction of the cave. The second soldier quickly followed but stopped at the entrance and stood there confused, too afraid to enter.

Father ran towards the papal soldier by the cart, swinging his axe in a circular motion above his head. The soldier stepped back. Father stood between him and the prisoners. Holding the axe high, he quickly with his free hand grabbed his large knife from its sheath attached to his belt. He cut the ropes that tied a prisoner's hands. She grabbed the large knife from him and cut the ropes around the hands of the other women and their children.

'Quickly go home, she screamed to the bewildered folk.

Father looked into a small boy's wide, terrified eyes. 'Run now as fast as you can,' he said, and once again swung the axe keeping the soldier from stopping them. 'Who do you think you are,' Father yelled. 'You have gone too far, this time,' he threatened.

'Look at that,' the papal soldier screamed. 'The peasant swings his axe like it's a twig.

I am out of here,' he yelled as he ran.

'So am I,' screamed the soldier guarding the entrance of the cave. 'I have been told these mountain people are witches and have demonic powers.'

Father noticed a large book opened on the ground and picked it up. *'It's the Holy Bible. It looks to be written in Latin. The cover is in polished leather. The horsemen in scarlet probably lost it when their horses were nervous and jumping about,'* he thought. *'Who are they, and what do they want of us?'*

Father crept across the broken-down walls of the ancient fort. He held the large very heavy book the best he could in both arms. He entered the cave, which led into a smaller room about eight feet square. From this room were openings into two underground tunnels.

'Marco where are you? Are you down one of these tunnels?' His father called.

'Shoosh, Papa, I am here,' Marco replied as he walked through the dark, towards him. 'You wouldn't believe it, but I followed the nuns and listened to their conversation. I am glad we learned Latin at the 'School of the Barbs, as they spoke in this tongue. I suppose so the children wouldn't understand what they were saying. One of these tunnels leads to a convent in the village. That is where they have taken the children. The other leads to another part of town where the Catholic Church stands.'

'Nooo,' groaned Papa, 'they will be lost forever. The children will be brainwashed and will never return home. To have this so close to our villages and homes is terrifying. From now on our children won't be safe. Only God knows the extent that they will carry out their agenda. Oh, God! Please save us,' he wailed.

CHAPTER 22

PISA

*P*ietro sat marking papers when a knock was heard on his door. It was sergeant Farel from the Royal Medici Army.

'Buongiorno Pietro, I have letters for you from your folk. Are you holding your Sabbath service in the hospital's solarium this Saturday?'

'Si, will you attend Farel,' Pietro asked, knowing the consequences for the sergeant if he was caught and for all of them if it came to that.

'Si Grazie, can my family attend as well?

'Si at 10 am.'

'Grazie. Arrivèderci, Pietro.'

Pietro's heart skipped foolishly, as he walked to the window and quickly opened Judith's letter. As he opened the pages, pressed wildflowers fell to the floor. He carefully picked them up, pressing the petals to his nose. Homesickness overwhelmed him as he smelled the scent of the mountains.

> Dear Pietro,
> The Bambina has arrived. We've called her Ruth. You should see her Pietro; she is so beautiful. After seeing little Ruth, the memory of her birth father is now fading. Mamma has helped me make the swaddling

clothes. Maria helped by knitting a rug. Papa over the freezing months made a beautiful rocking chair, for me to sit on when feeding Ruth. He also made a bed for Maria. Next week we will all be sleeping in the summer quarters. They are the large bedrooms on the other side of the villa. You know the ones, which have the large double doors that we can open through the summer nights. Maria will have her own room, as Ruth needs to be fed at night. Marco has just come back from the 'School of the Barbs.' He has been helping papa plough the fields and plants the summer crops. When I'm feeding Ruth, I can see from the parlour window snow on the mountain's tips, everything else is brilliant green. I never get tired of the mountains, they're so beautiful, and your family is so kind to me. I can't thank you enough Pietro for befriending me. I miss you so much.

Judith.

Thank you, Lord, for keeping them safe, he sighed.
Pietro also received a letter from his father.

Dear Pietro,

I have some very startling news for you. The Duke of Savoy, as you know is the owner of our mountains and valleys. He allowed the papacy to open their Catholic Church and monastery in Torre Pellice. They are capturing our signoras and bambinos and dragging them into a cave that leads to their buildings, and there isn't a thing we can do about it. Thank the Lord our little village is many miles from that dreaded cave. Trading at the markets in Torre Pellice will be out of the question for the rest of the family. The family is now hemmed in, and our village has become a real ghetto. To warn others, the signoras are teaching the bambinos a rhyme. It is called Little Red Riding Hood. It means that it is dangerous in the woods and if the children enter, they will be dragged off to La Finta's place. The bambinos are now being taught this story everywhere, and not just in our mountains. It's to teach them not to enter the woods on their own or to talk to strangers.

Love papa.

PIETRO SAT THINKING about his father's letter. *'If they were here in Firenze they would have more freedom, but this city is too licentious. It would be like taking them to Sodom, and if caught witnessing, which they would, of course, it would be the same here as it is everywhere. I will be glad when my contract is completed and I can go home,'* Pietro thought.

Strolling through the hospital gardens Pietro met Carlo and Enzo, walking toward the hospital wards, for their daily visitation.

'Buongiorno Pietro,' they both greeted.

Pietro nodded.

Carlo walked next to Pietro with his head down twisting his moustache in his fingers as he spoke quietly. 'We must meet and tell you about our medical visitations in the homes, and our success in witnessing to these folk.'

'Si,' that's right,' whispered Enzo grinning. 'Si, Pietro they have agreed to join our group for Sabbath worship,' he laughed, throwing his hands out wide.

Both Carlo and Pietro laughed at Enzo's enthusiasm.

'That's wonderful. Arrivèderci for now,' Pietro grinned, as the others went into the hospital.

SABBATH MORNING PIETRO looked at the new converts crowding into the garden room. There were rich educated citizens, as well as their servants. All wanted to hear what he had to say.

He stood in front of his congregation praying quietly for the Holy Spirit to guide his words. The sermon went well and he finished by saying, 'I wish to remind you that Christ is your hope and glory. He died on the cross for your sins. They are washed away with His sacrifice. In Romans 6:23

we are told. 'For the wages of sin is death, but the gift of God is eternal life in Christ Jesus our Lord.' Believe this and you will be saved. In 1 John 1:9, it says 'If we confess our sins to Jesus, He is faithful and just to forgive our sins and to cleanse us from all unrighteousness.' We must listen to God and His word in His Holy Bible and not to man and his traditions. Now let's pray.'

GERARDO KNEW THAT Pietro held Sabbath meetings in the hospital's solarium. He stood back in the shadows of a large oak tree listening to Pietro preach.

Gerardo thought, *'Why do you Waldenses push your religious point of view on everyone? You are stubborn people. What you have just preached, Pietro will get you into a lot of trouble. You have just interfered with the structure of our economy, with your preaching, and that won't do. Don't you realize the papal system needs indulgences to run their churches, and we need the papacy's money for our banks? It's not important what is taught to the peasants, as they are very superstitious people and believe mostly in folk laws. Penance suits them, as indulgences suit us. No person, of high or low birth, is interested in the Christ you keep preaching about. Why can't you worship amongst your own, as the Jews do?*

Gerardo stood shaking his head. He moved closer and looked in the back window of the conservatory. He was shocked, and thought, *'Look at all these people. There are some very important citizens attending these meetings. I must keep a better eye on Pietro.'* He moved away until the meeting was over, and then approached Pietro on the garden path.

'Pietro, I was looking for you. I am leaving for Rome, and I will meet you in two weeks. Don't worry as I have a letter from Lorenzo, and will take it to the Pope. It's for your safe passage while in Rome.' He pulled the letter from his coat pocket and handed it to Pietro. Pietro read it carefully and then handed it back, happy his safety was taken care of.

'Grazie, Gerardo for your help. I will now be able to relax and enjoy your wedding, without looking over my shoulder.'

'Arrivèderci Pietro, I will see you soon.'

GERARDO TRAVELLING TO Rome went first to Pisa. He took only Sergeant Farel with him. 'Farel I wish to make something very clear to you. I was outside the hospital's solarium on Saturday and saw you and your family attending Pietro's meeting. You know, to attend those meetings is considered treason. If I report you, your family will be run out of town, and also the region. The people in other areas have been told to kill dissenters of the state. If you keep quiet about the things you see and hear on this trip to Rome, I will keep quiet about what I saw. Do you understand Farel?'

Farel nodded and looked away.

After several days of hard riding, they arrived at the city of Pisa. Gerardo alighted from his sweaty, tired mount.

'Take care of the horses Farel as I have business to attend to,' He ordered.

Farel watched Gerardo stride across the grassed grounds to the cathedral.

Cathedral in Pisa

THE POPE SAT QUIETLY in the large cathedral pew and looked around at the artwork and plain grey and white striped walls. He rubbed his soft jewelled hands together and leaned forward to listen to his friends.

Francesco Salviati Archbishop of Pisa paced in the cathedral isle and turned and spoke to a second person. 'Lorenzo's Firenze isn't a Christian city. They may have papal churches but the people in the city and even the state are Humanists. We need to bring them in line. They are influencing people across Italy with their great wealth and culture.'

Francesco de Pazzi, head of the Pazzi bank turned to the Pope. 'It's a disgrace that they didn't lend you the money Your Holiness, considering the Medici bank is the papacy's bank.' Being agitated he walked a few steps away, stared without seeing at a painting, and muttered under his breath. *'It has now left our bank struggling and more than likely we will never be re-paid.'* He cleared his throat, faced the Pope, and spoke louder so the Pope could hear. 'Now that you have bought the town Imola and its trade route to the shipping port, with the new taxes that you will receive, you should be able to quickly pay back your debt to our bank, Your Holiness.' He stopped and said no more.

The Pope was enraged by his forwardness. He stared at him, drawing his eyes tight. They looked like slits in his pudgy white face that now darkened to crimson. Both men thought he would start yelling or even worse, have a heart attack.

They all now sat silently in the pews busy with their thoughts, as they waited for the fourth person. Soon footsteps could be heard on the tiled cathedral floor. They looked around to see Gerardo approaching. Gerardo nodded and half bowed to the Pope, his future father-in-law.

The Pope spoke, 'Let us go into your private rooms Salviati.'

Archbishop Salviati rose and led them into a small office at the back of the cathedral, and when all were sitting, Gerardo still standing spoke.

'Your Holiness I've come as quickly as I could. I bare bad news. Duke Lorenzo has bought favour with the King of Naples, who has signed an agreement, through his son that is governing Imola, to allow Lorenzo to continue using the trade routes and ports. He will stand by his word Your Holiness. Also, the interdiction against Firenze must be lifted for all concerned Your Holiness. The King has stated that he wants Lorenzo at all the ecclesiastical functions. He feels that Firenze has a lot to offer. It may lead to war if we aren't careful.'

The Pope who had covered his papal gown with a black cape and hood now sat hunched over with his fists clenched, mouth tight, and eyes flashing. He looked like a black eagle ready for flight.

Francesco de Pazzi noticed His Holiness's anger and used it to his advantage. 'We must go to war with Duke Lorenzo, but how I don't know without upsetting the rest of Italy?'

The archbishop stood and went to the open window. It was high and all he could see were the rooftops of other buildings surrounding the church.

'I know how. We will kill Lorenzo and his brother Giuliano and place the bank and its books with another ruling family. One who respects your position Your Holiness, and one that will bring the city under your papal rule?'

Both now turned and looked at de Pazzi.

The Pope spoke. 'Si, an excellent idea, you do it, de Pazzi, then you will be the head of both the banks.' The Pope thought to himself. *And Lorenzo's family will never again own the Medici bank. I am so glad that I have been paid by Lorenzo for his son's position as future Pope, and his daughter's betrothal to my son. I will make sure that Pazzi's bank clears my debt as well.* A look of sheer cunning crossed his face. *Si this has worked out better than I expected.'*

The archbishop walked away from the window and sat. He leaned forward and spoke in a very quiet voice, describing how the murders were to take place. Unknown to all in the room, someone was standing outside.

CHAPTER 23

ASSASSINS

*P*ietro blew out his lamp. It was very late; he looked down the street and saw a man on the street corner.

'Is that the town crier?' Pietro wondered as he opened the window to listen.

'It's midnight and all is well,' the town crier called.'

'Si, I thought it was late; it has been dark for some time.' Pietro stretched and then saw a shadow moving towards his door.

The bell rang. 'I wonder who is calling at this late hour,' he thought as he went down the stairs. Standing at the door was a woman with her hood well over her head and partly shielding her face. 'Come in,' Pietro muttered. When in the hall with the door shut, she removed her hood. It was Sergeant Farel's wife.

'Pietro, I have a message from a kinsman in Pisa.' She then told him the tale of treason. While talking she reminded herself. *'I must be careful to carry out my husband's orders. I mustn't tell Pietro that he and Gerardo were in Pisa and that Gerardo has turned traitor. This information is far too dangerous for all concerned.'*

'Please Pietro, I can't tell you who gave me this information and you must promise that you won't tell Lorenzo, that I gave it to you.'

'Si, I promise.'

THE NEXT DAY A KNOCK was heard at the Medici Bank's door. Duke Lorenzo stood and absent-mindedly opened it.

'Pietro, please come in, and what can I do for you? Are you happy with your wages going into an account here at my bank?'

'Si, Your Lordship, but I haven't come to speak to you about banking, but something else. It's very important.'

'Sit Pietro, and let me pour you a drink. I know you don't drink seasoned wine, but I have some lovely fresh new wine from my country estate.'

Pietro extremely anxious started to splutter, 'Your Lordship you are in great danger, as they plan to kill you and your brother Giuliano.' He realized he had approached the subject the wrong way.

'How dare you, Pietro.' Lorenzo stopped pouring Pietro's drink and now spoke in a raised agitated voice. 'After all, I have done for you. You sit there speaking such nonsense. Who would kill me? Firenze is a powerful city and everyone is flourishing. And who would confide in you anyway? They would come directly to me on such a serious matter. It's just a hoax, that's all Pietro.'

Pietro sat quietly with his head down praying for the right words. Lorenzo stopped ranting and watched as he continued to pour Pietro's drink. He realized when Pietro sat like this, he was praying.

'And what does your God say?' he mocked.

Pietro took a deep breath and started again. 'Please scusare, I was over-anxious to tell you the terrifying news, your Lordship. I will start again. A certain citizen was visiting the 'Pisa Cathedral,' when they overheard a conversation between the Archbishop and Francesco de Pazzi in the Archbishop's office.'

Lorenzo interrupted, 'How did they recognize their voices, and who is this person?

'He heard them mention each other by name and the informer is fearful for his and his family's lives. I have been sworn to secrecy.'

'Go ahead then. Continue with your story.'

'The bishop suggested that they kill you and your brother. The other voice,' Pietro stopped.

'Well continue,' Lorenzo ordered, now very agitated.

'The other voice was the Pope himself. They called him Your Holiness and mentioned the papacy. The Pope suggested that Francesco de Pazzi should do it and then he could take over both banks. The bishop moved away from the window and spoke quietly, so they couldn't hear why, how, and when, but they wanted to warn you. Your Lordship, they were concerned for you.' Pietro decided to stop before he went too far.

'Si, I understand,' the duke muttered as he paced. 'Is that all?'

'Si, your Lordship.'

The duke walked Pietro to the door. 'Grazie Pietro and addio.'

The duke mused to himself as he paced. 'The story has merit as I know the Pazzis are just waiting to overthrow our family and to take over our bank. The bishop is jealous of the freedom we have and wants us completely under the papacy, and ah! The other man they called 'Your Holiness,' would have been the Pope himself. It certainly sounds like what he would do. He needs to stay in Rome and look after all those children he's fathering. He knows that Giovanni when old enough will take over the papacy and Firenze. We paid him well for the privilege, and then it will all belong to the Medici household.'

SEVERAL DAYS LATER Duke Lorenzo stepped out of his home office and nearly tripped over his wife's maid. She was crying and rubbing her swollen eyes with her apron.

'Gina what's the matter?' the duke asked, as he guided her into his office. When the door was shut, he gently drew her into his arms. 'Why are you so upset?' He kissed the top of her head. 'Is it our bambino? You did give him to my butler, who was to take him to my cousin's country manor, didn't you?'

She now sobbed even harder. 'My Lord, the Duchess knows about us. She was there at the delivery and said no one must know about the birth, as it will disgrace the Medici name. In the middle of the night, she made another servant take the bambino to the orphanage.' Now hysterical and sobbing loudly she collapsed into a chair.

'Now, now, it's all right, I will sort it all out,' soothed the Count.

'It's even worse than that, because someone wrapped our son in Medici swaddling clothes, and the Duchess is furious. She said I did it on purpose to let the citizens know the bambino belongs to the Medici family, and she said the citizens of Firenze will think the ruling family throws their bambinos away.'

'Did you wrap our bambino in Medici swaddling clothes?'

'No, oh no, I wouldn't do that to you,' she sobbed. 'I don't know how it happened. I was sleeping when they attended the bambino and that's when they took him away.'

'Well, we will collect our son straight away. Stand up and dry your eyes and come with me.'

Shocked nuns stood to attention when the duke and his household's servant girl entered the orphanage.

When in the nursery they were taken to a crib. On the crib in small letters was written 'Medici'. The Count leaned over the crib and tenderly picked up his son. 'Come let's go home; there's been a huge mistake made.'

The nuns watching started whispering. Sister Florien clapped her hands and all quickly turned and went back to work.

The count knocked on the Duchess's door holding his little bundle next to his heart, with Gina standing close behind. The door opened; 'I think we need to come in Clarice and discuss something with you.' They quickly entered and the door quietly closed behind them.

PIETRO SAT STUDYING passages from scripture under his flickering lamp light. It was late and he was tired; he stood and blew out the lamp. Looking out of the window he marvelled at the full moon's silver light on the city's skyline.

'What's that,' he thought. 'It looks like a large bat. He leaned forward straining to see properly. 'It's a young person in a black cloak. What's going on?' As he stared, he noticed many others following. He watched as they ran quickly, effortlessly across the neighbouring rooftops, with their cloaks flying behind them. The leader waited for the others to catch up. He then climbed cat-like down the building. Black silhouettes followed.

'Well, wait until I get my hands on them. It is so dangerous. What if they fall?' Pietro thought as he negotiated his stairs in the moonlight.

Pietro stood in the shadows and when the group of ten or more laughing, gesturing, youths stepped into the street light, without thinking of the consequences, Pietro held out his arms, barring their way.

'What am I doing? They are carrying swords and daggers, attached to their leather belts. Why aren't they attacking me? I must act tough.'

'What's going on? Pull your hoods back so I can see you better,' he commanded. *'Well look at that, my students from the hospital college,'* he thought surprised. 'Signors please explain?' He demanded.

'Doctor de Vaux, we have been told by our parents that our Duke's life has been threatened and we have formed a group and called ourselves the 'Assassins.' We take the watch each night, around the city's skyline. From up there, it's a good vantage point. Many more youths have taken up the cause and keep watch in different districts,' their leader explained.

'Come into my residence, and we can talk more about this,' Pietro suggested.

Pietro marched them up the stairs and when there, lit the parlour's lamp and endeavoured to stoke the fire's dying embers. They stood awkwardly, whispering amongst themselves as they looked out the window across the city's moonlit skyline.

Pietro looked around at his three chairs, shrugged, and continued. 'Please signors, do your parents know about this?'

'Si they do, and so does the duke,' their leader answered.

'I hope you're not going to use those instruments of destruction?' Pietro asked, nodding towards the weapons attached to their leather belts.

'The leader nodded and spoke. 'If we have to, we will.'

'But you are training to save lives not destroy them.'

'Well, we will only destroy a life if it tries to destroy our Duke,' he answered.

'How are you going to stay awake at the hospital?'

A big burly youth, known as Joss answered. 'The fresh air and exercise will clear our heads for the next day at the hospital, Signor de Vaux.

'Haw, haw, haw,' they all laughed.

Pietro nodded as it was useless to pursue the subject further.

CHAPTER 24

MURDER

Duke Lorenzo stood on the palace rooftop overlooking Firenze. It was early and the roosters' reverberating calls broke the morning silence.

He thought as he looked over his city. 'The Assassins will be home by now, and getting ready to go to mass, but the merchants preparing their stalls outside the cathedral, will keep watch.'

He looked down into the yard below and noticed his cavalry preparing for the day. 'I have doubled my guards, what else can I do? If you ask me, it's just a hoax, as everything is so peaceful. I must hurry and prepare to go to church before the citizens arrive.' As he watched he could see people entering the city gates and crossing the river Arno. He turned quickly and walked to the stairs.

Giuliano met him on the stairs. 'Buongiorno Lorenzo'.

Lorenzo nodded.

Giuliano continued, 'I have a few things to attend to. Go to church without me and I will meet you there as soon as I can.'

'Si, don't be too long. It's best to receive the 'Host' before the others arrive,' Lorenzo explained, as he moved down the stairs.

Duke Lorenzo entered the red-domed cathedral in Firenze. 'It's Easter Sunday and it's a high day for all my citizens.'

As he walked down the aisle, he looked around the

cathedral. *'Well, there are only two old men praying in the back pew, that's good; I will sit right down in the front. Perhaps I should kneel while I wait. They're ringing the sanctuary bells 'for the Elevation of the Host,' and the citizens will be arriving soon for mass. Blow where's that brother of mine.'*

Suddenly he felt a hot sharp pain across the back of his neck. *'Ouch, what's that?'* He placed both hands where it stung, and then he looked at his hands. *'Blood, What?'* Jumping to his feet, he swung around and saw the two old men from the back pew standing there, hesitant and uncertain. One held a sharp knife, which was now dripping with his blood. Immediately they turned and ran exposing their black garments.

'They aren't citizens, but priests. I don't recognize them. They aren't from here. I must get help.'

He staggered towards the back door, where the guards were standing. 'Don't stand there, I need help,' he yelled. They turned to see their Duke pouring blood. His clothes and hands were covered in blood as he tried to stay the bleeding. Pools of blood covered the floor where he ran. Now it seemed everyone was yelling.

Giuliano stood very still in the church's portico. The church bells were chiming loudly across the city but he heard something else.

'What's going on, someone is yelling. He thought. *'Oh no it's Lorenzo; something has happened to him.'*

He started to run towards the commotion when two men jumped from the shadows. One had a dagger and while the other held him, the dagger was quickly, violently thrust into his heart over and over and over again. He looked up at his attacker and realized it was Francesco de Pazzi. He could hardly recognize him as his features were so contorted. His arms thrashed back and forth in a frenzy of blood lust, stabbing him nineteen times. Stumbling, he turned around and saw Archbishop Salviati who had held him from behind, but now stood back. Giuliano tried to speak but blood filled his mouth, and he gurgled, spluttered, and staggered, falling dead upon the portico floor.

The two murderers ran from the scene. 'Quick let's go through this door, as it's the vestry,' Salviati explained. 'We can hide until it's safe.'

Citizens entered the cathedral's portico and stepped on something slippery. They looked and saw it was blood that now flowed down the steps. The women screamed, lifting their dresses and undergarments, as they grabbed and held each other so they wouldn't fall, while some of the men rushed to the dead body. Most drew back out of the portico. A terrified babble of raised voices, plus screams for help echoed through the empty church.

Salviati placed his outer robe over de Pazzi's blood-soaked clothes and they quietly left the vestry.

Pietro sat studying his Bible. He stood and opened his window. Leaning out he watched many fashionable carriages pull into the square. The citizens were arriving for 'Easter Mass,' while the cathedral bells chimed loudly across the city square. Pietro looked up smiling as he watched birds taking flight from the cathedral's tower.

Suddenly he heard screams over the bells and then saw two men cautiously step from the side door of the cathedral.

'That's Archbishop Salviati, and the other is de Pazzi, and they are the ones after the Medicis,' he thought.

Now panicking he lent out the window and saw a group

of students walking towards the cathedral. *It's Joss and his group of Assassins.'*

Joss looked up and saw Pietro waving. He couldn't hear what he was saying but noticed he was pointing frantically at two men leaving the side door of the cathedral.

Pietro watched Joss talk to the others. They all looked up. Joss waved and then they ascended quickly to the neighbouring rooftop and silently, stealthily, followed the conspirators below. The Assassins were once again negotiating the city's skyline.

Citizens in the town square watched the youth dart across the buildings. 'Get them,' shouted a man pointing to the two escapees.

Pietro ran down his stairs as quickly as he could. He was way behind the mob but able to see where they went.

The conspirators rushed to the Town Hall. They hoped to seize control of the city, but none of their colleagues in crime was there. As they stood breathless at the door, the Assassins jumped down on them, pinning them to the ground.

The city's citizens were close behind. 'Don't let them go,' a citizen screamed as they surrounded the conspirators.

Pietro now stopped running as he approached the crowd. He knew it was a scene he didn't want to participate in.

'How did I get involved in this,' he thought.

One of the approaching citizens shrieked. 'They killed Giuliano and tried to kill our Duke.'

'Let's take them upstairs and hang them from the windows, for all to see what happens to conspirators of the state,' shouted one of them.

They took them upstairs and seizing Archbishop Salviati

they tied a rope around his neck and lowered him out of the town hall window. He struggled, gurgled, and as he took his last rasping breath, he held up his fingers with a sign for all to see and died.

'Look at Pazzi, he is covered in Giuliano's blood,' another called.

'Strip the murderer's garments; strip him,' the mob yelled.

Francesco de' Pazzi was stripped naked and then hung from another window to dangle alongside the archbishop.

Pietro looked up at the hanging corpses and felt sick. 'This is what happens when you are on the wrong side of the government and that could easily be me,' he thought.

Joss stood also watching. Pietro placed a letter into Joss's hands. 'This is from Duke Lorenzo. He said if anything happened to them it had to go to his Cavalry Officer. It must be delivered quickly as it's most important. The officer will know what to do?'

Joss nodded and sprinted off. When at the barracks the officer immediately opened it. He nodded and spoke. 'This is a list of other conspirators living in this city. We must act now before they are warned,' he barked.

Soon Medici soldiers were searching homes across the city and eighty conspirators and their families were hunted down and killed. Citizens listened to the cries of the offending families as they were slaughtered, thus warning them all of the consequences of betrayal. Now the Medics were more powerful than ever before.

CHAPTER 25

OTTOMAN CAVALRY

Several days later Pietro mounted his horse. He was heading for Rome. 'Carlo you are in charge now, so take good care of the hospital until Doctor Solomon Michelini returns. I have finished my term here and will be going home after visiting Rome. Arrivèderci my good friends, and peace be with you,' Pietro called as he waved.

A large crowd had gathered in the Town Hall piazza. They cheered long and hard when Duke Lorenzo and his family stepped out of the courthouse. The family waved to their loyal subjects. Pietro walked his horse quietly behind the crowd and unseen by all including Lorenzo he waved to the royal family. 'I will see you at the wedding in Rome,' he muttered to himself. Drawing his cloak's hood over his head he cantered across the bridge and out of the city.

TIRED AND SADDLE SORE after two days of hard riding, Pietro sighted a troop of soldiers that were quickly advancing.

He thought. *'It's the Ottoman army and by the look of those horses, they're the mounted elite. Si scouts are sent before the regular army. I have been told they pillaged wherever they go. They seem to be going to Rome. Maybe they are riding as bodyguards for the Sultan. Perhaps he has business with the Pope. I must get out of their way. They are extremely dangerous.'*

Pietro took refuge near the road in a farmer's field. Tying his horse behind a tree he quickly hid in a crop of tall thick corn, and watched. All the soldiers were as one; their ranks were perfect. The horses' hooves made the ground vibrate as they passed with the sound of 'thud thudding thud; thud thudding thud.'

'Wow, what beautiful horses. Look how they hold their heads; Arabian that's what they are. Si, I have heard about them.' He thought.

Pietro watched the white horses with shimmering red cloths covering their flanks, gallop with little effort like they were gliding above the ground. The soldiers seemed to sit without movement on their mounts, while they held long lances in one hand.

He grinned as he watched and thought, *'In the wind, their metal helmets with those long, thick, white feathers on top, look like peacocks displaying their plumage and look at their breastplates, they shine like silver. I was told the metal is the best there is. How magnificent they are.'* Pietro sighed as he watched the long line of soldiers pass by.

Walking to his horse he thought. *'The Sultan isn't amongst them. This means the heavy cavalry will soon be following. I must take shelter somewhere before nightfall.'*

Pietro galloped his horse along the country lane. He was aware he needed to find shelter quickly as the sky was darkening and the evening promised to be moonless. He noticed a cottage across the field and decided to ask for help. 'Maybe they will let me stay in their barn for the night.'

Getting closer, he thought. *'I can see a light under the door, but all the windows are black.'*

He knocked on the door which opened immediately, and he caught his breath. In front of him was a circle of black-cloaked figures sitting on a wooden floor strewn with straw.

A man stood and walked towards him with a lit lamp in his hand.

'Scusare, could I please rest in your barn,' Pietro asked, turning and following the man who was already walking towards the barn.

'Si,' the man growled.

The man stood holding his lamp at the barn door and watched Pietro take his horse to the stables. Pietro removed his pack and quickly brushed his horse while it drank and ate.

He thought to himself while he worked. *'There are at least ten horses here. They must belong to the others sitting in the house.'*

All the while the man stood motionless by the door with the lamp in his hands. Pietro now turned and looked at the thick-set man.

The man spoke, 'Sleep here on this hay.' His voice was deep and gravelly, sounding like a growl when he talked. He pointed and left.

'I wonder who they are.' Pietro thought.

When the man went back to the others, he spoke to them. 'He's a Waldensian youth. He won't be any trouble to us.'

Pietro woke to voices whispering in the barn. It was still dark but he could sense the horses' almost silent movements and gentle snuffing in the stables. *'Horse thieves,'* he thought and jumped up without thinking of the danger. He drew his hood down over his face and quietly moved to the stable door.

'It's the cloaked strangers, and they are preparing to leave. How quiet they are while harnessing and saddling their horses. I wonder why they are so secretive'

He heard something behind him. He swung around. It

161

was the stranger with the lamp moving towards him. Soon the light shone on his face.

The stranger spoke to Pietro in his deep gravelly growl, but now somewhat kinder. 'It's alright, the visitors are leaving. Join me in the house and I will prepare some food, and we can talk.'

Pietro followed the stranger to his small dilapidated cottage. As he walked, he noticed the pinkish-grey sky and realized it was dawn.

'*Well, that must have been some gathering,*' he thought. 'Please Lord, watch over me,' he prayed.

When in the one-room cottage he noticed the two small windows were boarded up. The place looked deserted. He was very puzzled by what he saw. The man brought a mug of hot gruel from a pot hanging over low embers. He handed it to him with a chunk of hard dark dry bread.

'Grazie,' Pietro nodded taking the gruel and bread, easing himself to the floor.

The black-cloaked stranger also sat on the floor with his meal and dropped his head and prayed out loud. 'Lord, thank you for your protection over the work our brethren are participating in. There is so many poor that needs our help and to know your love. Please bless this food we ask in the name of God the Father, Jesus the Son, and the Holy Spirit,' he prayed crossing himself.

'Well, I am in the presence of a Catholic. I must be careful,' Pietro thought and then had his own silent prayer.

The man watched. When Pietro started to dunk his tough bread into his hot gruel, the man spoke. 'Don't be afraid. I realize that you are a Waldensian youth and you have been taught to be watchful at all times. My name is Franco. I'm also from a detested group of people. We are hunted for our faith the same as your people. We are monks called the Fraticelli de Paupere Vita. We were part of the Franciscan monks but separated from the order because we didn't believe in the Catholic Church's remission of sins through indulgences. We still consider ourselves catholic monks, but we don't belong to the church. We have our bishop; Bishop Nicholas, and he believes that we should be supporting the poor, not robbing them. We are hunted by the church as heretics the same as your people, and if they find us, they will put us to death. The community sees us as caring local people and they don't realize who we are. We worship in secrecy in the night and the men you met last night are some of these monks.' Franco looked around the room and continued. 'Nobody lives in this dwelling and as a Waldense, I know you can understand our predicament, and will keep silent on these matters.'

'Si, I do understand and I will keep your secret. My name is Pietro, and si, I am a Waldensian from the Piedmont Mountains.' Pietro continued. 'You need to know there is an Ottoman army passing this way. Their elite force passed through last night and the heavy Cavalry always follows a day or two behind.'

'Grazie, then we must move straight away.'

Tuscany Landscape

PIETRO WAVED AND RODE off in a different direction to his new friend. After riding most of the day he arrived at Siena. Pietro rode his horse up the steep cobbled path. He stopped and looked over a stone wall at the vivid sun-drenched rolling hills, vineyards, olive orchards, and country estates sprawling as far as one could see. It was a typical Tuscan landscape.

Soon he passed through shops clustered closely together. He came to a fork in the narrow path. The sound of a crowd yelling echoed down the narrow track. It was loud and frightening. He turned the corner and came across a group of Ottoman soldiers, outside the town's tavern. They were laughing and bellowing at two of the regiment's men who were fist-fighting.

'Get him, that's right,' one yelled.

'Look at that, a good one right in the face,' another yelled.

'It's the elite army, that I watched last night,' Pietro thought. I must go to the back of the Inn, without being seen by them, and try to approach the innkeeper for a room. If I come and go this way, they might not notice me. By the way, they are drinking and carrying on, they probably won't notice anyway.'

He tethered his horse behind the Inn and passed a lone soldier sitting on a bench near the path's wall. The soldier was looking over the sprawling landscape. He looked up and watched Pietro enter the inn.

The innkeeper took Pietro to a small room at the back of the stairs. 'Si, you are a doctor. We have a sick man in this room. Si, you must take a look,' he said with much pointing and hand gesturing. 'I will get one of my workers to care for your horse.'

Pietro nodded.

'Grazie Doctor de Vaux,' the fat grubby innkeeper said grinning with relief, as he waved his hands about; crossing himself and rolling his eyes to heaven. He then hurried back to his patrons.

Pietro entered the small room with its large fireplace in the corner nearly taking up the whole room. In the bed was a rotund man with a long white beard. He had a ruddy complexion, and his blue eyes were bloodshot and hazy. He had a fever.

'Hello, my name is Pietro and I'm a doctor. The Innkeeper asked me to have a look at you.' After examining the large sweaty man Pietro gave him some herbs, for his fever and spoke. 'Take these herbs in a pot of hot water.

Drink often and keep warm Signor and you will be well in a few days.'

'Grazie,' the stranger murmured.

Pietro went outside to a faucet for water that ran into a horse trough. He leaned over and washed with his mother's homemade soap, made with herbs to kill germs. The young soldier sitting at the bench watched intently.

Pietro hurried back to the Innkeeper to explain the sick man's needs. 'He needs lots of hot water to drink with his herbs, and he needs it often,' Pietro explained.

'Si,' the Innkeeper nodded. 'I will now show you to your room Signor,' he said with hand gesturing towards the stairs. He walked ahead of Pietro up the stairs to a nice large room.

Pietro nodded to the Innkeeper, 'Grazie,' he said, and the Innkeeper left.

Pietro walked to the window and sighed.

'*Si, very nice,*' He thought, as he looked over the back courtyard and the breathtaking country views.

Pietro looked down at the soldier still sitting on the bench. '*He looks familiar. I must go down.*'

CHAPTER 26

AN OTTOMAN SOLDIER

*P*ietro sat on the bench next to the soldier. 'Splendido, huh.'

The soldier swung around and stared at Pietro. 'Si,' he nodded.

There was something about the soldier. He certainly wasn't a Turk and he wasn't Roman. He looked more French or even Swiss. Pietro spoke slowly in his Waldensian tongue. 'Can you understand me?'

'Si.'

'You look like you are from the Vaudois clan.'

'Si.'

Pietro was now very puzzled. *'Does he understand what I am saying,'* Pietro wondered?

'From the Piedmont Mountains north of here,' Pietro explained.

The young soldier screwed up his face and thought as he tried to work out Pietro's words, and then spoke slowly as if he were trying to remember how to speak in the patois tongue. All the while using his hands to poke or punch the air in front of him. 'Si — family — from — mountains — shared Bible — army killed them. I became a slave.' He now started to speak more fluently. 'I was ten years old. The army has its slave unit called the Kapikuku, where I was placed and made to train very hard. When I was fifteen years old, I was placed in the Janissary unit, which is the elite unit in the infantry.' He spoke haltingly with a strong Turkish accent. We are the Sultan's household troops and bodyguards,' he said proudly.

Pietro nodded. 'Do you remember the mountains?'

'Ah the mountains,' a look of sadness came over the soldier's face. 'Si, they were very beautiful. I remember the snow on their tips, and the running brooks and the grass it was so green. I dream of it often,' he said with great sadness and longing in his eyes as he splayed his hands in front of him. 'I was very young when my family left the mountains and went to other regions as missionaries.'

'What was your family's name?' Pietro probed.

The soldier fumbled about in the lining of his uniform and pulled out worn, carefully folded pieces of paper. 'These are the only pages of the Bible I was able to save. I am still a Christian. They think they have converted me to Islam,' he said. On the top of each page was his name. He handed it to Pietro.

Pietro noticed the Bible verses were written in the Waldensian Vernacular. This gave him a real start. '*I must be careful he may have stolen these pages from someone.*'

He read out loud, the name slowly. 'Gionn de Vaux.' Pietro sat bolt upright. 'What is your papa's name?'

'Francesco.' I often say it out loud so I don't forget how to say it.'

'My name is Pietro de Vaux. You are my kinsfolk,' Pietro said shocked.

The soldier jumped up 'Si, my family spoke of you often. We are the same age and I remember we attended church together.' Now laughing, but also crying, he grabbed Pietro who stood up and hugged him back.

The memory of his lost relative flashed through Pietro's mind. '*Si he looks very similar to our Marco,*' Pietro thought as he stared at the soldier.

He now laughed and sniffed back tears of joy and surprise. 'My parents spoke of your family. Your papa was indeed Francesco. He was my papa's brother.' Pietro said, once again hugging and slapping his cousin's back. 'Will you come back with me to the mountains?'

'I don't think so,' then as an after-thought, he continued. 'No, I have to stay with my troop. I am the captain, and we have very important news, we must convey to the Pope,' he said, now regaining his composure. He placed the paper with the Bible passages into his coat lining and spoke. 'Would you like to walk with me to the town piazza, where my men are racing their horses? It's just harmless entertainment for the locals. There is a good Inn at the square, where we can have a meal.'

While they ate, Gionn explained his life to Pietro. 'You know I have also been trained to be a medic, for the army and when not at war we are the Sultan's policemen and firefighters. Our main duty is to guard and care for our Sultan.'

Pietro could see he was very proud and somewhat happy with his position.

Pietro thought, *'It's certainly much better than being murdered for your faith. But I wouldn't give up witnessing about my Jesus for anyone.'*

Soon the horses assembled outside the Inn. The locals now gathered and Pietro and Gionn joined them. Five horsemen lined up for the race. Ribbons and bells were woven into the horse's plaited manes and tails. The crowd, the cavalry, also the riders and horses all stood still and waited in excited expectation.

Siena's Piazza, where they raced horses

Suddenly there was a bugle call, and all the horses were off. The crowd roared as they pounded past. They turned with a swerve and a slew of choking dust, covering Pietro and Gionn. The skid of hooves and the jangle of bells sounded as they turned and raced down the next stretch. All were spectacular as they seem to fly, and not touch the ground. The soldiers sat straight and proud. They turned another corner and all were in line; all were uniform in their gait. There was a dust cloud over them, and then suddenly a horse in the pack was pushed against another and it stumbled. Soon other horses lost their balance and tumbled over each other, leaving only two horses leading the charge.

Citizens rushed down the track and Pietro and Gionn followed. They had minutes to move them off the track before the others were around for a second time.

Pietro and Gionn examined the soldiers but they weren't hurt, as their helmets were strong, and they were experts at safe falling. Their horses stood by fidgeting and snorting. Suddenly the two riders came around for the second time. The citizens roared and threw their hands in the air. Both horses finished neck to neck and Pietro realized as he watched that all five horses would have done the same, as they were trained to work as a team.

Gionn laughed heartily. 'Surprise, surprise,' he whispered. 'We all knew this would happen, as the horses are trained to keep in line on the battlefield.'

THE NEXT MORNING PIETRO woke to someone calling. 'Pietro de Vaux, get up you sluggard.' It was a Turkish voice speaking in Patois.

Pietro knew instantly who it was. He went to the window, laughing. The sky was dark grey with pink on the horizon. It was still very early. He called out. 'Where are you going cugino?'

'To Rome, Arrivèderci cugino,' waved Gionn as he galloped away with his troop.

Pietro dressed and crept down the rickety stairs. He sat at their favourite bench and read his Bible tracts. They once again gave him great peace. He prayed, 'Lord you have cared for me the whole time I have been away from home. Thank you for taking care of Gionn. If it's your will Lord let us meet again, and impress Gionn to come home with me? Thank you for your care over my loved ones at home, and

Lord, please keep me safe while I travel to Rome. In Jesus name, I pray. Amen.

Pietro turned to see the large ruddy man that he treated the day before, coming from the barn.

'Buongiorno friend; are you well enough to leave your bed?'

'Grazie Doctor de Vaux. I am fine,' he said as he climbed onto his gig. I never had a chance to introduce myself. I am Bishop Nicolas, and I believe you met the monks from my order the other night. As a Waldense you will understand the importance of my work,' he placed his finger to his lips, 'and the necessity of secrecy.' He smiled a jolly smile and his kind blue eyes twinkled. In the gig were bags of food, and clothes.

'Take care and stay warm, so your cold doesn't freshen,' Pietro instructed.

'Si, don't worry about me. To do well to others will warm my soul,' he said as he drove away with bells on his gig and horse, jingling in unison with the warbling of birds in the nearby trees.

As Pietro watched him drive down the lane he thought. 'It's hard to believe he is a Catholic Bishop. He's so open and certainly doesn't dress like them, but that's probably the idea as he doesn't want them to know who he is.'

CHAPTER 27

ROME

Rome's Colosseum

After riding for several days Pietro arrived in Rome. The city was a historic museum with old crumbling buildings as far as he could see. Soon he rode past the famous 'Circus Maximus Arena.' It was very long, and once had seating for over three hundred citizens. Here the Roman charioteers raced in front of cheering crowds. In his mind, he could hear the crowd yelling, and the chariots jostling each other, with wheels grinding together, as they fought for victory or death. On the other side was the Jewish ghetto, still a hive of activity, with people going about their business.

Soon he passed through the Arch of Titus.

He looked up at the historic carvings and thought. 'This is the oldest archway in history.' He caught his breath when he saw the huge Colosseum in front of him. Involuntary shudders went down his spine.

'I hope Gerardo is here to meet me,' he thought.

Approaching the Colosseum, he looked up at its crumbling exterior. 'Papa said it was struck by a violent earthquake over one hundred years ago. Many said it was God's judgment on the Roman people, and all the evil that this building represented. Si, it's certainly a mess.' He thought as he looked up at its walls. 'I can't believe its size. I will go in and sit and wait for Gerardo.'

As he sat, he contemplated the scenes that would have taken place. *'Christians were falsely accused of the most dreadful crimes, the same as today. I can see them in the arena kneeling together praying for a quick death, while they tried to shield their little ones from seeing the wild dogs or lions circling them; ready to tear them into pieces.* He looked up to where the seats would have been. *'Si, they would have laughed and cheered. Whole families cheered at the horrific spectacle, as God's holy people waited for death.'* Pietro shuddered, as he saw the scene in his mind. He stood and walked back to the entrance and looked for Gerardo.

Gerardo walked up to Pietro, who was staring across the ruins, deep in thought. Gerardo placed his hand on Pietro's shoulder. Pietro jumped and swung around as Gerardo spoke.

'It's an awesome historic place, ancient Rome, isn't it? I would have loved being here at the time of the gladiators.' Gerardo confessed without thought of Pietro's feelings.

Pietro felt sick in the stomach. *'Gerardo doesn't understand*

*my beliefs and that means trouble for me. Fool, fool, fool, that's
what I am,'* he thought.

THEY RODE TOWARDS THE Vatican. All around them
an angry crowd swelled in size as it marched to Saint Peter's
Basilica Square. They yelled for answers. Soon the Pope and
his cardinals appeared and they walked proudly, confidently,
through the raging crowd, who parted to let them pass into
St Peter's Cathedral.

The Pope benignly smiled at them. 'Bless you, my
children,' he said, as they knelt one by one kissing the hem
of his robe, as he passed.

When appearing on Saint Peter's balcony he held up his
arms and the crowd's angry roar, changed to a loud cheer.
He possessed great charm, and his dignity and presence
were always impressive. It rarely failed to arouse devotion
from almost all who came in contact with him.

He now spoke. 'Do not worry my faithful subjects. All is
well and we are now at peace with King Ferdinand of
Naples. We have settled our differences, but if any problems
again arise, there is a very strong adversary against Naples,
here on our docks. They have different grievances with the
King from us, but they will keep the king in line. It is the
Sultan of the Ottoman Empire, who right this moment has
his ships in our Vatican docks.' A cheer went up. He raised
his arms and waited, and when all was quiet, he continued,
changing the subject completely. 'The celebrations for the
wedding of my daughter Teodorina to Gerardo Usumari,
nephew of Duke Lorenzo of Firenze will start tomorrow.
Please enjoy the festivals that will take place over the next
two weeks.' The crowd cheered.

TEODORINA SAT AT HER window. She had watched earlier the raging crowd moving through the streets towards the Vatican, and now as she worked at her embroidery, she could hear the bells of 'Saint Peter's.' She knew Mass was in the process because she could hear the sound of the chanting voices.

Gerardo quietly unnoticed by the Pope led Pietro through the long-covered fortified corridor. It went from 'St Peters' to 'Castle Sant'Angelo.' When in the castle's rooms he quietly knocked at a door and then entered.

'Pietro, how good it is to see you,' laughed Teodorina as she walked up to him, and greeted him with a kiss on each cheek.

'Grazi,' Pietro responded, feeling much happier.

'I have a room further along the corridor for you Pietro. Gerardo is sharing it with you, so don't worry you will be safe there.' She looked at Gerardo, who smiled and nodded. 'He has promised to protect you, while you are here with us in Rome,' she grinned at Gerardo, who was grinning foolishly, as he watched her every move with love and devotion. 'Now let's eat, and we can relax and catch up with our news later.'

Relaxing in the parlour while they listened to a court musician Teodorina whispered to Pietro. 'Leonardo da Vinci wants you to go with him to visit the peasants tomorrow. I believe many need a doctor.'

With all his previous apprehension dispelled, Pietro nodded and sat back to enjoy the evening.

PIETRO ROSE EARLY the next morning. He noticed Gerardo had already left or maybe he had never been there.

Pietro dressed and sat at the window reading and praying. A maid knocked on the door and entered the room with food.

'Grazie,' Pietro murmured, as he quickly pushed his scriptural papers under his cloak, hoping she didn't see them.

The maid left quietly, bumping into Teodorina who was talking to others in the hallway. She stopped to whisper to Teodorina and then disappeared down the hall.

Pietro finished his meal and stepped out of his room. He left the cloak and his Waldensian clothes behind in his pack, as to wear them while in Rome was far too dangerous. Today he wore his brown suit, which was suitable for his profession. He realized that it was best to dress like this while in Rome.

He noticed Teodorina in the courtyard with a large group of children. They were all talking and laughing at the same time, trying to tell their story first to her. When she saw Pietro approaching, she spoke to the children.

'Now, go along my darlings, the nuns are patiently waiting for you,' she laughed, waving her hands, shooing them on.

Pietro watched fascinated by her devotion to all these small children, who now walked noisily through the large courtyard with several nuns. He couldn't help but notice the difference between the nuns' plain black uniforms and Teodorina's ornate golden gown, which was heavy with pearls.

She greeted him with laughter and teasing. 'Well look whose here, it's doctor sleepy head. Leonardo is waiting for you in Vatican square. Come with me and I will show you how to get there along our covered walkway.'

Pietro followed, 'Teodorina, where did all those small children come from?' he asked.

'Oh, they live here. They are some of my siblings. The older ones are away at school. Didn't you know 'His Holiness,' my papa has many children, and they live in this castle? His Holiness quarters are here as well. For the next three days, he and Gerardo will be away on business. When they arrive home, you will see lots of celebrations here in 'Saint Angelo Castle.'

Pietro was horrified and thought, *'I must leave before they get back. What am I doing in such a place? What was I thinking? I must have lost all reason while compromising with the worldly in Firenze. These aren't my people and can't be my friends, as they don't love the truth and someone or something must give, and it will be my neck. Dear Lord this is what happens when one has a foot in each camp. Please forgive me for my foolishness.*

CHAPTER 28

LEONARDO

'L'eonardo, there you are,' called Pietro; all the while fearful and looking about as he rushed towards Leonardo with his medical bag in his hand. 'I'm in a hurry. Perhaps you can visit these people by yourself and then report back to Gerardo.'

Leonardo shook his head, 'They won't let me in their hovels without a doctor. It won't take long Pietro, and they do need you to look in on them.' But Leonardo's real intention was to sketch the poor and needy. He found they made such interesting subjects.

Pietro approached the first hovel. 'Buon'giorno, Signora; my name is Doctor de Vaux. Can I assist those ailing within? Also, my friend with me is Leonardo da Vinci; Rome's most famous artist. He needs sketches of local people for his work in the Vatican. Can he sketch your family members while I administer to your sick?'

'Si, si come in.' The Signora grinned, beckoning with her arms.

She turned to others in the small, dark, dank room 'It's that famous artist from the Vatican. He has come with the doctor,' the Signora laughed and talked quickly, pointing in the direction of the Vatican and swinging her arms as if she was painting on its walls.

'Si it's him.' Another Signora laughed and waved her arms about as she spoke. A lot of arm waving and excited, fast-talking to and fro took place in the hovel. Everyone talked, all at once. Many other locals crowded into the building, hoping they would be sketched and become famous.

Pietro attended the Signor that lay on a straw bed in the corner of the room. 'If you use these herbs,' he pulled out herbs in a small container from his medical bag and handed them to the old Signora. He turned and continued to talk to her husband. 'It will help you to overcome the fever,' he explained. He spoke quietly as he administered to his needs.

As they walked to another dwelling, Pietro had a quick look at Leonardo's sketches. Pietro noticed how Leonardo had drawn Signora's long curly unkempt hair and large nose. He drew another with a deep hook in their nose and a jutting-out bottom jaw.

Pietro explained to Leonardo, 'That jutting out jaw is caused by very badly aligned, rotten teeth, protruding past the top festering canines. I had to minister herbs for pain caused by those teeth,' he sighed.

Leonardo also sketched the old scraggy Signora with her toothless grin. Others he sketched with deep-set eyes, in gaunt faces.

'Oh, dear Leonardo, si they are on the whole ferociously ugly people. Your sketches are true to life, but I don't see them that way. I see them as poor lost souls needing a Savior. Their features have been developed from generations of neglect and poverty,' Pietro sighed as he spoke to Leonardo, without thinking of the consequences.

Leonardo grunted, preferring not to have heard the comment about needing a Savior. He now stayed outside the hovels that Pietro entered, and drew the rich Roman citizens as they passed by on horseback or coach. He drew them with more wholesome features, but mostly his drawings were of his composition, enhancing even their long noses and thin faces. Some were pudgy and fat, but all with very Roman features.

When Leonardo decided to go back into the hovel, he noticed Pietro was praying with the sick and quoting scripture as he spoke of Jesus' love for them. Leonardo knew to quote scripture without a priest was against the law but at that moment he didn't care as he was more interested in sketching Pietro's face.

He thought, *'I must sketch Pietro while he is ministering to the sick. He has so much compassion and kindness; I must see if I can capture his expression on paper.'* Leonardo's charcoal stick moved quickly and expertly across the page, as his penetrating eyes and alert perception gave depth and beauty to the drawing that none other could depict. He sketched Pietro's face that had no marks or wrinkles, and his nose that was long and straight, and his long hair falling straight to his shoulders and parted in the middle.

'I must capture Pietro when he speaks about his Jesus. Look how his face lights up and his eyes shine with great happiness. Peace and joy radiate from his very being. I can see that Pietro trusts his Jesus against great odds.' Leonardo's charcoal stick raced across the page. *'I hope I have captured the pure love shining on Pietro's face,'* he thought.

He was aware that he was witnessing something very special and realized he had never seen this expression on the faces of the church leaders.

Vatican with the castle bottom left amongst trees next to the river

LEONARDO'S HORSE WAS tethered to a hitching rail, outside St Peter's square. He turned and explained his movements to Pietro. 'I must also hurry as I need to ride some distance before nightfall. I'm travelling to Milano and the journey will take over a week. I have been commissioned to paint 'The Last Supper,' on the refectory walls in the Dominican Monastery. Arrivèderci my friend,' he said.

'Arrivèderci,' mumbled Pietro, who now rushed back through the hidden corridor to his room in the castle. He needed to quickly pick up his belongings and head to the Vatican stables. Fear now overwhelmed him. He felt quite sick. He had to hurry before he was noticed.

When in the room he couldn't find his bag. *'Someone has been here and removed my bag with my clothes and my cape with the bible verses. Oh no, I'm in real trouble. Lord, you had impressed me all day to go straight to the stables and not come back to my room.'*

Pietro walked through the castle's corridors as quickly as he could.

'Don't run; try and look as if there isn't anything wrong,' he thought. *'Who's that coming behind me? They seem to be in a hurry. I will look out this window and pretend I'm not worried and perhaps they will pass. Help me, Lord.'*

Pietro's hair stood up on the back of his neck, and his spine tingled. He drew a deep breath and looked around.

'Giovanni, what are you doing here? I thought you were in Firenze,' Pietro said, somewhat pleased when he saw thirteen-year-old Giovanni, Lorenzo's son, quickly approaching him.

'I'm staying at the 'Cardinal College,' here in Rome,' Giovanni answered.

'So, you are training to become a Cardinal?' Pietro responded, relieved.

'Doctor de Vaux don't my clothes show you who I am? I'm already a Cardinal.' Giovanni was wearing the habit of the Vatican Cardinals. Pietro was surprised and nodded. He turned and walked on with Giovanni trailing close behind. They soon came to the Vatican stables and Pietro turned to speak. Out of the corner of his eye, he noticed Giovanni waving his arm beckoning the Vatican guards to come. They pulled their swords from their sheaths, and ran up to Pietro, flicking their swords in a threatening way.

'Sorry Doctor de Vaux, but we must go immediately to St Peter's,' Giovanni said, standing tall and full of self-importance.

The secret walkway from St. Peters to the castle

As they walked through St Peter's Basilica, Pietro listened to the sound of their shoes clicking across the marble tiles. He noticed the large statues and beautiful paintings. The building was huge and made him feel small and insignificant. Pietro shook uncontrollably as fear crept over every fibre in his body.

'Jesus, I trust you in all things. It's my stubborn heart that has brought me here, he whispered under his breath as they walked along a side passage that now led them to a meeting room. Giovanni knocked on a large ornate wooden door and then quietly entered. The guards pushed Pietro forward into the room and then slammed the door behind him. Pietro sucked in his breath. Sitting in front of him, behind tables set in a semi-circle, were thirty-nine cardinals.

'Is this Doctor de Vaux?' a very old cardinal asked.

'Si Your Eminence,' Giovanni answered and then sat, at the end of the table.

The aged cardinal thin and bent now spoke to Pietro. "Is your name Pietro de Vaux and are you a Waldensian from the Vaudois clan in the Piedmont Mountains?'

Pietro's legs nearly collapsed under him. 'Si,' he answered.

'Some of the poor in our great city have reported you. They said you have been sharing Bible texts and praying with them, without the presence of a priest. Is that true?'

'Si, Your Eminence.'

'It has also been reported that you carry written Bible text hidden in your cloak.' Is that also true?

'Si Your Eminence,' Pietro murmured and then silently prayed. 'I am in your hands, Lord.'

'You do realize that it's considered treason, and you will be put to death?'

The other cardinals with their quills scratched down the conversation.

'Si Your Eminence,' Pietro answered, holding his head down while they accused him, and all the while he prayed.

'I don't know why such an educated person like you, would willingly go against the Pope. He has been given authority from God, to be the visible head of the universal church, and he is considered to be part of God's deity here on earth. Also, I am interested to know how such ignorant mountain peasants like your kinsfolk, can stand constantly against our divine authority; facing generation after generation of being hunted to death. Why, can you tell me this, why?' he screamed, thumping his hand on the desk.

Suddenly Pietro looked up. God was speaking to his mind. 'Pietro your people have been hunted to death; yet their blood has watered the seed sown, and it failed not. You have been born for such a time as this.'

His face white with fear now shone with the Glory of God. He looked up to heaven. All sat quietly and watched. The recording cardinals placed down their quills. If all in the room could have seen the other dimension, they would have realized the room was filled with evil angels, gloating over the procedures taking place.

Pietro now spoke. All heaven listened as God's angels surrounded him. 'Cardinals we have been taught in our villages, that our education is to be for God's service. It's our duty to send out missionaries to scatter the precious truths. It's in scripture and scripture alone, that we're to place our trust. Jesus only can forgive and save us. Our only offence is not to worship God according to the will of the Pope.

The aged cardinal sat stunned by the truth that was spoken quietly and reverently. It resonated in his mind and penetrated his heart. Slowly colour rose from his neck upwards, covering his whole face. He was furious and now screamed. 'Get him out of here; the dungeon and the burning pyre for him, and the quicker the better. Who does he think he is? Not even kings stand here and speak to us like that.'

CHAPTER 29

THE VATICAN PRISON

*D*eep in the earth's bowels, far below castle Sant'Angelo was the Vatican's prison. It was a place of extreme torture. Screams and cries of the afflicted echoed constantly through the dark dank cells.

The Vatican guards now dragged Pietro from 'Saint Peter's Basilica,' down through the underground tunnel to the castle's prison. Pietro passed all the tortured souls, festering in the hell hole. Their stench almost suffocated him. They walked further on, to another very gloomy chilly place, as they didn't want Pietro to be seen or heard by others, until the appointed time. Opening large metal doors, they threw him in.

Pietro sat quietly praying for wisdom and strength. It was silent in his cell, then someone coughed and another moved. Pietro realized there were others present.

'Who's here?' Pietro asked. All answered at once. Some in Patois and some in the Romano tongue.

'How many are there in this cell?' Pietro asked.

'Seven now counting you,' a strong deep voice answered. Pietro knew this to be one of his brethren by his dialect.

'My name is Pietro de Vaux from the Piedmont Mountains,' he answered.

'You're from the village Borgata Cyrus a woman answered. 'I know your Mamma well. I am Susan Joaquin and was from La Torre, but now I live in Rome with my husband and family. Thankfully the children were visiting others when they arrested us.'

Another voice answered' 'Si, my name is James Joaquin, Susan's husband. We were witnessing in this city when they caught us.'

'A deep older voice now spoke, 'Pietro I am your Barb, Daniel Reveilli. I was making arrangements for the Joaquins to return home to La Torre when we were caught. There are many people from all over Italy attending the wedding of the Pope's daughter. Fires will be lit in Vatican square plus the Seven Hills of Rome as part of these special celebrations. The Pope's soldiers are capturing all the Waldensian brethren here in Rome. We are to be consigned to these flames as a spectacle, to deter others from following our so-called heresy. They say they don't want us to wake fanaticism in their region with our preaching.'

While the Barb spoke, Pietro moved across the dingy cell to his voice. He felt for the man and then fell into his arms. 'I'm a fool. I have trusted in man. I thought they were my friends but all the while they were setting a trap. How foolish I've been.'

Soon the others moved to where Pietro and his Barb stood and all talked at once hugging and reassuring Pietro.

After a while, they quoted memorized Bible verses, and then sang in such a way, as only one can, when renewing and fortifying their faith before death. Tired and isolated the saints pleaded their cases before their Lord. Not a sound could be heard outside their cell. Not a speck of light was seen. Death at this moment didn't occupy their minds, but how they stood before the throne of God. They pleaded for any unknown sins to be forgiven, and that Jesus their High Priest in the heavenly court, to present their cases. They prayed and sang and fellow-shipped together.

Time stood still; there wasn't any way of telling day from night. After some time, a light could be seen way down the long dark passage. It came closer and closer. Soon a guard stood at the door with another.

'Pietro de Vaux, Pietro de Vaux, come forward immediately,' he barked

Pietro stepped forward.

'Are you Pietro de Vaux?'

'Si.',

The door was unlocked, and Pietro was pushed forward into the brightly burning torchlight. After being in a pitch-black cell, without even a shadow to be seen, the light blinded him and he couldn't see the men's faces. They dragged him down the passageway to a small room with daylight streaming through its high window. The guard pushed him down onto a chair in front of a table. Pietro looked up at the other man armed with ink and a quill, while he placed the paper in front of him.

Pietro caught his breath. It was his friend Farel. Now reassured he spoke. 'Sergeant Farel, what are you doing here? Is Gerardo back?'

Farel looked at Pietro as if he didn't know him. 'The captain has sent me. I am travelling back to Firenze and he thought you would like to write to your family before you go to the flames.' His expression was very guarded.

'Si,' Pietro nodded. Icy fear crept over every part of his being.

He thought to himself. *So, Gerardo is giving me a chance to write to my folk. I wonder if he's sending a message with Farel for the others in Firenze.*

Pietro placed his quill into the ink and wrote.

Dear Papa and Mamma,

I have been sentenced to the flames. Mamma, please don't cry. I promise to be brave and strong. You would be proud of me if you knew the things I have done, but time doesn't allow me to tell them.

Papa, I've done as you have taught. I have presented the Holy Scripture to lost souls. Everywhere honest and good people have been subject to crime and vice, which is prevalent throughout the regions. They are seeking a better way and are accepting the Bible truths, and Jesus as their Savior.

Marco, God has commissioned us to do this wonderful work and there is no other way. Be faithful my brother and we will meet on the sea of glass.

Judith, I didn't get a chance to tell you, that I love you. Stay strong in Jesus.

Little Maria, don't be sad, because we will all be together on that great resurrection day.

Love Pietro.

When in the stables Sergeant Farel read Pietro's letter, and wept. 'Please Lord, let there be a miracle. Pietro has been deceived by his friends.' Farel now rode as fast as he could to his destination, and away from the terrible events to take place.

CHAPTER 30

MARTYR PYRE

Several days later, Sergeant Farel arrived in Firenze. He walked his horse over the Ponte Vecchio Bridge that crossed River Arno. He was occupied with his thoughts and didn't notice the citizens socializing and trading in their gold shops. When on the other side, he mounted his horse and rode into Firenze's piazza. Suddenly flies buzzed around his head. They seemed to be coming from above. Looking up he realized he was sitting under a dead person, swinging by his neck from the Town Hall's second-floor window.

Leaning over he asked a citizen, 'Who's that person; he looks to be a Turk, and what's his crime?'

'Oh! He is Baroncelli and was one of the conspirators that were trying to kill our Duke. He escaped to Istanbul, but our soldiers followed him and brought him back to receive his punishment. Now he hangs alone, for all to see his shame.'

Farel moved on quickly, as the Black Plague had become prevalent amongst the poor in Firenze. He also needed to find Carlo and Enzo before he went home.

As he walked through the hospital gardens, he thought, 'It's mid-afternoon, so their classes should be finished by now. Perhaps I will find them in the garden conservatory.' To his relief, both were still there discussing hospital procedures.

'Buon'giorno, Carlo and Enzo.'

Both men looked up. 'Buongiorno Farel,' they both

192

greeted.

Carlo spoke, 'We didn't know you were back from Rome.'

'Si, when did you get back?' butted in Enzo, rushing forward and hugging Farel, with lots of back-slapping.

Carlo followed, precipitating a group hug, laughingly.

'I've come from Rome,' continued Farel somberly. I have a message from Pietro.'

Carlo noticed Farel's tired, anxious expression. 'Have you been home?'

'No, I came straight here.'

FAREL HANDED CARLO THE unsealed letter from Pietro. As Carlo read, he looked shocked and went deadly pale.

Carlo looked around at Farel. 'Have you read Pietro's letter,' he asked in a somewhat choked fashion.

'Si,' Farel answered dropping his head, as tears of sadness threatened.

Carlo turned to Enzo with tears running down his cheeks. In a hoarse whisper, he spluttered out the news. 'Pietro — is to die in Rome tomorrow — on a martyr pyre.'

Enzo paced, throwing his hands above his head, he cried out, 'I told him not to go to Rome. He trusted Gerardo far too much.' He now leaned right over pulling his hair. A painful howl, like from a wounded beast, escaped his lips, and he collapsed on the floor in a crouched position sobbing.

Carlo held out his hand and pulled Enzo to his feet, hugging him. Both men cried on each other's shoulders. After some time, Carlo spoke. 'We mustn't go on like this.

We know Pietro will enjoy heaven for eternity. We have been brought up to believe this is to be our lot. Let's pray. All three men prayed together, renewing their faith and gathering strength from their heavenly Father.

They sat together in the conservatory, as melancholy overtook them. The sun dipped in the sky, and the trees in the garden threw shadows across the windows, now darkening the normally bright sun-lit room.

Farel suggested, 'I think you should tell Doctor Michelini what has happened and resign from your post immediately. You need to go home and share with Pietro's family the sad news.' He stood and walked to the door. 'I must go home and sell all we have and move also. There are going to be big problems soon, here in Firenze. Duke Lorenzo is making all sorts of arrangements in Rome. When Giovanni takes over the papacy as the next Pope, which will be in a few short years, eradication will be on the agenda for all that refuse to follow him. At the next Sabbath gathering, I will warn all the folk so they too can leave for safer places. Where I don't know, as it seems the whole world has become informers.'

The youth walked with Farel and watched as he untied his horse.

'Arrivèderci;' they called and waved.

'Si, arrivèderci,' replied Farel, as he quickly rode home.

PIETRO WAS LED FROM his dark cell into the bright hot sunshine and marched with the prisoners to Saint Peter's. There was a feeling of excitement and gaiety amongst the people, as they crowded into the square. Small boys pointed and pulled faces at the prisoners; Pietro dropped his head. Others in the crowd looked away, disgusted to be in the presence of dissenters, traitors, here in their holy city.

The prisoners stood there waiting. Waiting for what, they weren't sure; perhaps for the crowd to settle or for the Pope to appear. Pietro felt weak and faint, and his legs could hardly hold him.

'I wish my head would stop spinning,' he thought. *'I am so hungry and thirsty, but my friends with me are older than I and have been in prison longer, so they will be worse off. I wish I could help them but of course, that's impossible, and after all, we will soon be no more, so what's the use,'* he thought.

After what seemed hours an Ottoman band could be heard approaching the square. There were cymbals, bells, and trumpets making the melody with the kettle drums tapping the beat. Soon they were in the square. Each player was dressed in bright, different-coloured silk robes, and all wore high-ribbed hats.

As they marched, they made a passageway through the crowd and around the martyr pile, not yet lit.

The guards moved forward marching their prisoners one by one, standing them in front of their stake upon which they were to be martyred, and then the guards stood between the prisoners and the crowd.

Pietro, as he stumbled forward thought, *'The piercing sound of the instruments hurts my head. I will hold it down and not look into the sun that may help. I won't look at anything, especially the pyre. It's just better to pray.'*

The band still playing now faced Saint Peters. The royal family, His Holiness the Pope, Gerardo with Teodorina, and Giovanni came onto the balcony. The Pope raised his hand and all became quiet.

Pietro looked up. Staring through hazy eyes he thought,

'Well look whose back and by the looks of things today I'm to be martyred by my friends. Please, Lord, help me to be brave.'

The Pope prayed and then he and the balcony party sat in their designated chairs. The Pope raised his hand once again. Kettle drums sounded and beautiful horses ridden by Ottoman soldiers, marched into the square accompanied by the band. All the while Pietro closed his eyes and prayed.

The horses' heads were held down, and their tails swished as they pranced with their front legs held high. One leg up, tap-tapping, tap, the drums played, then the next leg up, tap-tapping, tap. It was more of a dance than a march. All together they pranced around the pyre, and then they turned to the crowd and the horses bent one front leg while holding the other out straight, they bowed. The crowd cheered.

They continued around the pyre dancing, prancing, and twirling, with the drums tapping vigorously and the instruments playing a bright marching tune. The crowd clapped and cheered. The Pope was also mesmerized by the beautiful beasts and their upright cavalry riders.

Now the band marched out of the square playing their classical Turkish music. The horses still in the square started to run. They ran faster and faster around the unlit pyre. The lead soldier rode close to the prisoners and the others followed, forcing the guards to jump out of the way. Suddenly the soldiers' grabbed the prisoners one by one, swinging them onto their horses. The other horseback soldiers now formed a barricade on each side of the horses that held those escaping, and all rode out of the square three abreast. It took some time before the prison guards realized what had happened; even the Pope's party thought it was part of the parade.

As they galloped away Pietro feeling faint, slumped against the rider's back. With gratitude, he spoke in a hoarse whisper to his rescuer. 'Grazie kind Signor, God be with you.'

'When are you going to keep out of trouble cugino?' Pietro's cousin spoke in Patois with his strong Turkish accent. He now threw his head back and laughed heartily.

'Gionn!' Pietro cried.

CHAPTER 31

SAVED

After some time the horseback riders and their escapees arrived at a fork in the road.

Gionn pointed to the pine woods. 'We must turn and go in that direction,' he called. 'There will be wagons waiting to transport the prisoners away from this area.'

The soldiers turned their horses and galloped behind Gionn. When nearly on the other side of the woods they came to a large thatched roof building which they cautiously approached. Gionn knocked on two huge doors which were immediately opened, by a short rotund man with long black, curly, unkempt hair and coarse woodcutter's clothes.

'Quickly come in; si your horses as well. We don't want to be caught do we,' he said looking about before pulling the heavy wooden doors shut.

They entered what seemed to be a barn. Four scraggly bare-footed boys of various ages took the horses. A large grubby woman at the far end of the building placed dishes on a long homemade table. They looked to be the woodcutter's family and this seemed to be a barn -cum-dwelling.

'Please join us for the evening meal,' the woodcutter said.

They sat and the family stood waiting to serve. After grace, they were given loaves of bread which they tore into crusty chunks and dunked into bowls of hot vegetable soup; all the while talking at the same time with lots of hand waving and gesturing.

Their Barb Daniel Reveilli stood, and all became quiet. 'When it's dark I will go back to Rome with James and Susan Joaquin. They need to get their children before we leave. We should be back, God willing before sunrise.' All became quiet as they once again contemplated the fearful situation, they were in. Some silently wondered if the others going to Rome would unwittingly bring trouble. The Barb continued 'Let us link hands and pray together. Only God can save us.'

PIETRO WOKE SUDDENLY. He could hear voices; lots of voices. He lay there trying to remember just where he was. The soft, pink light of early dawn, filtered through the partly opened barn door. 'Si, now I remember,' he thought. Suddenly staring down at him were three very grubby, tear-stained faces.

'Now come along children,' whispered Susan as she guided her little ones to the table. Please sit still, we mustn't wake the others must we,' she explained as she shared with them the crusty chunks she saved from the night before.

Pietro stood and stretched. The soldiers were moving about and attending to their horses. When the children finished eating their bread, they watched fascinated with all the activities in the stable.

Suddenly the woodcutter pushed the barn doors wide open. 'Come along we must move quickly before the Vatican soldiers arrive. We have two carts outside waiting. They will take you away from here.'

When outside four escapees climbed into the first cart and lay side by side. The Ottoman soldiers heaped piles of straw upon them in the hope they wouldn't be discovered.

Each held their arms up to protect their faces and made sure they had a spot to breathe through. The children with their parents in the other cart did the same, while they were being covered with straw. The woodcutter with his oldest son in the second cart now nudged their horses to move forward.

'Pietro,' called Gionn. 'Last night I purchased from the woodcutter a pony for you to ride.'

'Grazie cugino,' Pietro replied without smiling, as he watched the carts rumble along the path and out the other side of the woods, into the open fields and the early morning sunshine. 'Please Lord, help us all,' Pietro muttered.

THE THUD THUDDING thud of horses' hooves could be heard as the Ottoman cavalry passed farmers in their fields and shopkeepers in their small villages. People rushed from their shops and cottages to watch the magnificent, white, Arabian horses gliding along in unison. Their mounted soldiers held long lances in one hand and wore breastplates that shimmered in the sunlight. Their helmets feathers fluttered in the breeze. All watched breathlessly, but what was that? The people stared at the strange sight. In the middle of the troop was a small black pony with its short legs galloping to keep in time with the cantering elite cavalry horses. Sitting on the pony was a Signor dressed in a plain brown business suit. He sat bareback with legs dangling, as he jerked awkwardly up and down on his mount. Who was he they wondered?

Soon the cavalry passed more pine woods and old Roman ruins, and then they approached the large Ostia Port at the mouth of the Tiber. Here the most advanced sailing ship belonging to the Ottoman navy graced its dock. Gionn and the soldiers cantered to its side. A special gangplank was lowered and set in place.

Gionn yelled orders to his men. 'Soldiers walk your horses one by one onto the gangplank. Careful, that's right. Steady, go slowly now. Don't scare your horses.' The horses walked onto the ship and down into its bowels. Pietro sat watching. He was the last to go.

'You will be fine, just walk the pony slowly cugino.' Pietro stepped off the horse and held its bridle tight and the reins in the other hand close to the horse's face as he walked onto the gangplank and down to its stables with the other horses.

AFTER SEVERAL HOURS THE ship sailed out of the port heading south in the Tyrrhenian Sea.

Pietro felt seasick as he stood on the forward deck. The ocean dipped and rose and so did Pietro's stomach. Leaning over the railing he vomited and then again, the ship heaved and dipped.

'Cugino, you look terrible.' Gionn laughed, slapping Pietro on the back. 'Come with me, the captain has requested your presence and he just might have a cure for your problems,' Gionn suggested as Pietro hung over the railing once again to vomit.

Pietro caught his breath when he stepped into the captain's cabin. Standing in front of him was an elderly person in full uniform.

The captain spoke. Let me introduce you Pietro to Prince Mehmed our Sultan.' Pietro bowed his head. Your highness this is Pietro de Vaux, your Cavalry Captain's cousin.'

Gionn bowed and spoke, 'Your Highness my relative is

unwell. Would you please excuse him as he needs to rest?' The Sultan nodded amused, as he could see that Pietro was suffering from sea sickness.

The captain poured a drink and placed it into Gionn's hands and nodded to Pietro. The glass was pressed to Pietro's lips and horrible as it was, he drank, daring not to do otherwise.

'Brandy to settle your stomach,' whispered Gionn as he led him out of the room. When in their cabin Gionn spoke of his Prince while helping Pietro to bed. 'Prince Mehmed is one of the most learned and brilliant Sultans ever to live. He has conquered and controlled Southern Italy for many years now, which makes the papacy panic, but the Sultan has been busy maintaining Istanbul and had not worried about the Italian provinces. Even so, the Pope keeps a friendly front when the Sultan is docked in this port.'

'Did the Pope and Gerardo visit your Prince in the last few days?' Pietro questioned.

'Si, and that's how I found out about your plight, so I talked the Pope and Gerardo, into letting us conduct the concert. They wouldn't have refused with our Sultan witnessing the conversation. Of course, they didn't know what I had in mind. Also, they didn't know we were cousins, and that we had already met.'

Pietro felt warm and fuzzy. The drink had made his stomach relax and now he couldn't keep his eyes open.

Gionn tidied Pietro's clothes and continued with his commentary. 'Do you realize the people in Istanbul were pivotal in starting the Humanist movement throughout Europe and especially in Firenze with Duke Lorenzo? The Firenze council had signed with our government an agreement to take up these idealisms. The Pope refuses to be outdone by the leading cultures of our time. This is why he keeps such a friendly profile with our leaders, even though our religions differ.' He stood and quietly left the room because Pietro was asleep and he was talking to himself.

The Captain and his First Mate were enjoying idyllic weather at the wheel. They had been conversing for some time. The navy band was playing for their Sultan, who rested in his cabin. The First Mate walked around the deck. Horrified, he noticed Moroccan warships were advancing at a rapid pace, and the lead ship was nearly upon them. He rushed back to the captain and took over the wheel.

The ship's bell sounded long and loud warning all aboard of an attack.

The captain bellowed. 'All hands on deck. All hands-on deck.' Sailors climbed and unravelled sails, trying to manoeuvre the ship for flight, but it was heavy and slow compared with the Moroccan small ships.

The lead Moroccan ship sailed close beneath the bow. They intended to board the Ottoman ship for hand-to-hand combat. A sudden gust of wind whipped up choppy waves causing the ships to separate, giving enough distance between each ship for the Ottoman navy to use their secret weapon.

CHAPTER 32

WARSHIP

The jerking of the ship as it separated frightened Pietro, as he lay in his bunk. He had been listening to the captain's orders and thought as he fearfully contemplated the events. *'The Ottoman ships are the only ones with cannons. I hate to think what's going to happen to the Moroccan navy.'*

The First Mate now steered their ship into position. Hidden weapons suddenly appeared from the deck's gun ports. On the given order from the captain who now paced back and forth, the guns fired and jetted smoke in huge billows. The noise was fearful.

As Pietro listened, he distinctly heard the crash of splintering timber. He cautiously crept onto the deck, yet he saw no evidence of damage. The scrubbed decks of the enemy ships appeared unstained by blood.

The captain once again shouted, 'All gun's fire,' and as the guns discharged, their reports turned into a rolling percussion, louder and more prolonged than any thunder. The flames made the smoke momentarily lurid. Some balls struck their target, and an enemy ship aflame, now slowly sunk in front of amazed but terrified sailors.

The Ottoman's First Mate turned the ship in line with another enemy vessel, and a broadside was shot. Pietro quickly returned to his cabin and prayed as he listened.

The captain yelled once again. 'Gunners aim well.' The guns crashed back against their breech ropes and smoke surrounded the enemy's fleet. One ship's forward mask was

204

splintered, and it crashed down and fell across the deck below.

'Gunners reload,' the captain bellowed.

In the grey smoke of cannon fire, enemy ships fled and were well out of range, when the terrifying gaggle of cannons bellowed across the waves. Soon, all that could be seen were small white specks of fleeing enemy ships in the distance.

Their ship peacefully continued its journey, and after many days of fair weather and good sailing, it turned into the Adriatic Sea. Their first port of call was to be Venezia. Here they would purchase merchandise to sell and trade.

SOON THEIR SHIP SAILED into the Venetian Lagoon. It was marshy in places and the Captain and his First Mate carefully navigated their passage. They moored their ship two miles from Venezia.

Pietro hung over the railing, intrigued by a small fishing boat that sailed by. It was filled with people. As he looked, he thought the people seemed very ill.

Gionn walked up to Pietro and laughed as he slapped his back. 'Cugino, do you still suffer from sea-sickness?'

'No, I have found my sea legs, but I was looking at those people in that small ship. What's wrong with them? They look seriously ill.'

Gionn looked very concerned as he spoke. 'Si, they are citizens, contaminated with the plague. The Venezia council has set up a very new hospital on the island of Lazzaretto Nuovo, and the diseased are restricted there until they are well or dead. The disease is different this time and is in the form of pneumonic plague, but the Black Plague has started again across Europe and is coming this way in many forms. They say we have only seen the beginning of things here in this port. It is increasing in strength, and when it reaches here, it will be as bad if not worse than last time.

As he spoke, another small fishing vessel passed, and this time it carried, many corpses, from the hospital island, and the stench was intense.

Pietro covered his face and drew back. 'Have these people died of the plague, and where are they taking the corpses?'

'Si, they did,' Gionn answered and continued. 'They are to be buried on the Island of San Giorgio Maggiore. This is known as the island of the dead. We must be very careful when we go on shore.'

Pietro looked at him shocked.

'Well, you do want to go home, don't you? Pack your things because the boat now approaching our ship, will take us to the port.'

Soon several official-looking men carrying cases and boxes alighted from their small vessel and walked up the gangplank onto the Ottoman warship.

Gionn whispered to Pietro. 'Since the last big outbreak of the Black Plague, over a hundred years ago, it has been a regular practice to check and fumigate foreign ships arriving in these ports. They believe the ships are bringing the plagues to their city.'

Pietro answered, 'I'm surprised that Ottoman ships are allowed to dock. I thought the Venetians and the Turks were at war with each other.'

'Oh! That is history. The Ottoman navy declared war on Venezia in 1453 and won the battle. The city has been under our control ever since and will be for years to come. We all now trade peacefully.

Gionn and Pietro returned with their packs and stood by the gangplank. The captain looked well pleased as he watched the disgruntled inspectors alight from his warship.

Gionn whispered as they followed the men down the gangplank. 'I think our ship has been given clearance which means our Captain will now be able to trade.'

Unknown to Pietro and Gionn, Prince Mehmed watched them leave and smiled sadly to himself. He loved Gionn as a son but realized Gionn was extremely homesick for the Piedmont Mountains, and now being with his kindred the prince knew he wouldn't return. 'Goodbye, my son. Thank you for your loyal service,' he murmured.

Gondolier and his gondola

SOON THEIR GONDOLIER was guiding their gondola down the Grand Canal. The sun was setting and it threw a pinkish glow over the city's skyline and dark shadows in front of the buildings. Amongst the shadows were silhouettes laughing and calling back and forth as they walked along the promenade.

Their gondola turned into a smaller canal and then into the Ponte dei Sopiri. Here many footbridges crossed the waterways leading to shops or boarding houses. As they sailed under one, rats scurried along the dark railings. Their gondolier skillfully guided their large boat passed shabby quarters. Suddenly he started singing a typical Venetian love melody. Windows above instantly opened and the young signorina's of the night appeared.

'Come up to us young lovelies,' they crooned down to Pietro and Gionn.

Pietro looked up. Women in bright clothes sporting large grubby wigs hung over the windows. Their faces were heavily caked in white makeup with bright red lipstick, making them look more like carnival clowns.

They waved and continued to croon. 'Come on, don't be shy, sweet face bambino,' they called to Pietro.

Pietro looked down, wishing not to encourage their attention.

Gionn laughed as he watched his poor embarrassed cousin. He called up to the women. 'Not tonight, Signorinas. We are busy and have some business to attend.

The younger of the two answered. 'You always say that sailor.' They giggled and shut their window.

Pietro with his head down noticed huge black rats scurrying along drainpipes that projected from buildings.

They seemed to be everywhere. He felt like gagging with the smell of the river and covered his nose. It was filthy with raw sewage and rotten food matter floating on its surface.

Gionn noticed and laughed. 'Don't fall in cugino. You will never recover.'

After some time, they stopped at a guest house with its doors very close to the river. They climbed up the few stone steps and entered.

'Pietro this is where we are staying for the night. I have a room here and they are expecting us.'

As they ate their evening meal, they watched through the open doors, young people dressed in brightly coloured clothes with elaborate party masks covering their faces. They twirled and danced as they passed over the neighbouring bridge, and then passed Pietro and Gionn. The city of Venezia was now fully awake, and the nightlife of festivals, parties, and balls had just started.

VERY EARLY THE NEXT morning while the Venetians slept, Pietro and Gionn stepped into their boat with their gondolier and headed to the mainland. After a short while, they arrived, and Gionn paid the gondolier. He then walked to a man on the roadside, holding two horses.

'Grazie Signor,' Gionn smiled and he produced more money.

CHAPTER 33

TWO YOUNG SIGNORS

People watched two young signors galloping past their barns, fields, and villages. One was dressed in a brown suit, worn by business signors and the other was an Ottoman soldier dressed in full cavalry uniform. One sat awkwardly, and one sat straight and regal, but both longed for the green pastures and mountains of home. They now rode as fast as they could to Milano.

GIONN AND PIETRO ALIGHTED from their horses and entered the Dominican church at Milano. There in front of them was Leonardo de Vinci busy preparing to paint a beautiful mural on the church wall. He had not long started and the characters were still sketches. There were many lines drawn, that came to a point in the middle of the wall. Moving closer they could see it was going to be a painting of 'The Last Supper.' He gave the feeling of movement by the way he placed the disciples and the use of different hand positions depicting the typical Italian way of speaking. He used a young man with short curly brown hair and some with long hair and beards. All were copies of sketches made while with Pietro in Rome. Pietro bumped against a pot of paint as he moved forward and Leonardo swung around. His face lit up, and then he saw the soldier with Pietro and he drew back.

Pietro grinned, 'Leonardo this is my cousin Gionn.' Both men nodded to each other. 'He has left the army and is coming back to the mountains with me. It's a long story and I will explain it all later.'

Leonardo quickly turned back to the sketches on the wall. 'Pietro do you recognize these drawings?'

'Si, they are the people you sketched in Rome.'

'What about the central figure?' he asked.

'Well, it's Christ, but I can't remember you showing me that sketch,' responded Pietro thoughtfully.

Leonardo just frowned but said nothing.

Two men appeared at the church door and watched warily. They were worried about the Ottoman soldier. Why was he travelling with the young man in a brown suit, but when they heard the young man speak, they realized it was Pietro. They cried out and rushed forward throwing themselves at him.

Gionn had stepped right up to the wall and was staring at the mural not noticing or interested in the excitement behind him. He looked hard at the main figure and spoke to Leonardo. 'It's Pietro, isn't it?'

Leonardo nodded placing his fingers to his lips.

'Si,' responded Gionn. 'Pietro looks just like that when he talks about his Jesus.'

Suddenly Pietro was slapping Gionn's back and talking to him. 'Gionn these are my dearest and oldest friends, Carlo and Enzo.'

The two men wiping the tears from their faces now grinned. They started to talk all at once; Enzo with lots of hand gesturing and laughing, and Carlo twisted his moustache while he talked.

Leonardo then spoke. 'Come let's go to my room and we can catch up with all your news.'

Enzo stood by the window and stared at Pietro. 'I can't believe you are here,' he said laughing, holding his hands out wide. 'You know, we too only arrived today. We were heading home to deliver your letter to your folk.' He turned and picked up his cloak lying across a chair and pulled the letter from its lining.

Pietro jumped up and laughingly snatched it out of his hands. 'Let me have the pleasure of tearing it into small bits.' When he finished, he threw the bits in the air, and they fluttered down upon their heads like large snowflakes.

'A new beginning,' he laughed.

'A new beginning,' his friends responded.

'Praise the Lord my family didn't receive that letter. God's divine appointments are always on time.'

Over the evening meal, Pietro shared all his news, and how he met his cousin Gionn. Gionn spoke in Patois but mostly in the Romaunt tongue, which they all spoke fluently. Then Enzo and Carlo shared their sad news.

Carlo spoke, but he was worried about Pietro's reaction when he heard the news.

'The Duke of Savoy has been told by the Pope, to clean up his territory. He has to rid himself of dissenters of the church. His soldiers have been pursuing barbarian attacks on the Waldensian people across Italy.

The army is now filled with murderers and ruffians, from off the streets. They're killing people, by using cruel and horrible methods. The army entered Alessandria and the deaths were great. Most were put on the martyr pyre. Paul Geymarli and his wife were trying to escape and were caught in Lucerne. Paul was attacked and left to die. He shuddered and dropped his head. 'I don't know what happened to his wife,' Carlo said twiddling with his moustache, trying to calm himself.

Leonardo cleared his throat and in a hoarse, emotional whisper spoke. 'I saw the posse carrying one of your friends on a pike, as a standard from town to town for all to see.' He stood, walked to a table in the corner of the room, and busied himself with his sketches.

Pietro asked. 'Do you know who the person was?'

'Si, she was one of the people escaping from Rome travelling in a cart. I believe her name was Anne Charbonnier.'

All in the room were silent. They were too shocked to speak, and they knew without asking, that terrible things would have happened to the others in the carts.

That evening they knelt together in fervent prayer; Leonardo didn't join them.

IT WAS EARLY AUTUMN and the breeze was chilly. Pietro sat on a bench listening to the rustle of leaves in the great oaks. He looked up from reading his Bible verses to marvel at their golden and red colours as they softly fluttered to the ground. He felt so homesick but also very upset about the news of his friends. He now bowed his head in gratitude for his safe- keeping and prayed.

Carlo approached him and spoke. 'Scusare Pietro, but I forgot last night to hand you a letter from your folk. It came after you left for Rome.'

'Grazie Carlo,' he answered and sat there thinking of home as Carlo walked back to the church.

Pietro thought to himself when he looked at the letter. 'It's in Judith's handwriting. A feeling of relief and a need to sob in Judith's arms came over him. 'Judith would tell me to pull myself together if she knew my thoughts,' he thought smiling. He opened the letter and read.

'Dear Pietro,

We haven't heard from you for some time. I hope all is well. Papa and Marco are picking the last of the vegetables and nuts and fruit for the season. The weather is changing and it will soon be winter again. Mamma and I have been busy preparing food to store in the cellar. Little Ruth is growing so quickly. She is now six months old. She has cut her front teeth and is eating mashed vegetables. Maria is always carrying her around on her hips. Mamma worries it might damage her back as Ruth is heavy. She is a very happy Bambina and tries to join in with our talking. She throws her hands about and talks away in baby language. She is so funny. Papa and Mamma love her. They are both well. Maria wants to know when you are coming home. Pietro your internship has now finished, please come home to us, as we miss you so much. I miss you terribly and pray for you daily.

Judith.

Pietro sat there thinking of his family. He realized he loved Judith, and couldn't wait to see her and the baby. Gionn stood at the church door watching him and when Pietro looked up, he thought, *'Gionn is coming home with me and Judith might like him better. I had better get in first. Oh, dear! Pietro, you are jealous. That will never do. Pull yourself together.'* He shook his head and smiled at himself.

CHAPTER 34

TORINO

Soon it was time to leave and all four men saddled their horses.

'Arrivèderci, Leonardo,' they called and waved.

When they arrived at Torino, they noticed a crowd moving towards the castle piazza. They tied their horses to the railing and moved with the crowd into the square. Carlo had given Gionn his long cloak to cover his soldier's uniform, in the hope they wouldn't be such a spectacle.

To their shock, it was to be an execution on a martyr pyre. 'Who's going to the flames today?' Pietro questioned an onlooker.

The woman was very glad to tell the story. 'He is Bernardo Ochino, a pastor from Sienna. He came and preached to the people in the valleys. After preaching for some months, he decided to return to his native town Busco. He was apprehended by the monks from his town, and condemned to death here in Torino.'

While they talked, a man with guards on either side entered the castle piazza. He walked up to his pile and while they tied him to the stake, he addressed the vast multitude.

'Remember we are only here for a short while. We are pilgrims on a journey to a better place called heaven. Be faithful and don't fear death. Jesus is your King and He loves you.'

The people were in tears with his calm, love-filled approach. After this, he began to sing with a loud voice and continued till he sank amid the flames.

Angels watched and recorded the events as they comforted the weary saddened people. God's people felt His presence and his peace rested upon them. The others in the crowd felt fear or just gloated.

Pietro felt so weary, but also very grateful for his deliverance. He wondered if he would have been as brave. The scene made a tremendous impression on him. All present that day could see heaven shining on the face of the man who sang.

SOON THE FOUR WERE approaching Pinerolo. They had been silent all day with their thoughts. When they entered the town they rode through the streets, and stared up at the Waldensian Cathedral perched on the hillside. It looked grand in all its glory and was a silent testimony for all far and wide.

Pietro spoke. 'When I was in Rome, Daniel Reveilli told me that if he returned home, he intended to preach about 'righteousness by faith in this cathedral. Let's see if he returned safely and if he did preach.'

They walked their horses up the steep incline. Tying them to the hitching rail, they stared at the magnificent views over Pinerolo and the surrounding countryside. Behind were tall mountains. They entered the church but nobody was to be seen, and then they heard someone moving about in the next room.

Pietro walked quietly to the room and found an old lady sweeping the tiles. 'Scusare, could you tell me if Daniel Reveilli is about.'

She looked frightened. Looking around to see if anyone

was listening, she spoke. 'He preached here when he returned from Rome. Through the week rough-looking soldiers waited and ambushed him and — um —.'

An old man walked into the church. 'Tell him what they did, right here in our town, for preaching in our Waldensian church.' He continued himself. 'They took our Barb into the woods. He had his tongue torn out for praising God. I believe he is being cared for by his family in Bobbio.'

All stood there completely shocked.

The old man spoke. 'All the towns in Piedmont, under one of our Barbs, have had brethren put to death.'

When outside by the hitching rail, they stood together in prayer, begging the Lord to give them courage and renew their faith. They then rode out of town, weary with sadness.

Cave where they hid

ENZO VERY UPSET SPOKE waving his hands about as he rode. 'Si, they seem to be plucking us off one by one and we are just sitting back and watching them kill our brethren.'

Pietro answered, 'If we return an eye for an eye and a tooth for a tooth, and go out and hunt them down one by one, as they do to us, we are no better than they.

Carlo spoke, 'I remember our folk speaking about a whole community being martyred. They told us so we would stand up under persecution.'

Pietro thought for a moment and answered. 'Si, I remember it was in the valley of Loyse on the French Border. They were quietly pursuing their daily labour when suddenly an armed force approached their valley. Despairing of being unable to resist them they at once prepared for flight.

Driving their herds before them, they began to climb the rugged slopes of the mountains. About halfway up, there was an immense cavern in which they placed their women, infants, cattle, and sheep. The able-bodied men placed themselves at the entrance of the cave.'

'Si that's right,' Enzo butted in. 'I remember now the story; my Mamma told it to me. She said we were never to be afraid and that we have to stand up for ourselves.'

Pietro continued with the story. 'The soldiers followed them and ascended the mountain on the other side, and approached the cave from above. They were let down by ropes from the precipice overhanging the entrance to the grotto. The platform in front was thus secured.

Enzo butted in again. 'Si, my Mamma said that the

Vaudois could have cut the ropes, and killed their foes, as they were being lowered one by one, but they were paralyzed by the boldness of the maneuver and they retreated further into the cavern.'

'At the cave's entrance,' Pietro continued, 'the soldiers piled up all the wood they could collect and set fire to it. A huge volume of black smoke began to roll into the cave, leaving the unhappy inmates the miserable alternative of rushing out and falling by the sword; or remaining in the interior to be stifled by the murky vapour.

Some rushed out and were massacred, but the greater number remained until death slowly approached them by suffocation. When the cave was afterwards examined, they found the bodies of four hundred infants suffocated in their cradles or the arms of their dead mothers. Altogether three thousand Vaudois, including the entire population of the valley of Loyse perished in that cave.

'Carlo now spoke, 'Our brethren told us this story so we'll stand together in adversity.'

'Si, si,' replied Enzo with much nodding. 'That may be so, but we need to do more. Enough is enough. We'll all perish if we allow this to continue and then who will tell the world about the Bible? Our Synod is due next month. We must discuss with our Barbs what's happening and what we should do.

CHAPTER 35

PRISONERS

Soon they arrived at Torre Pellice. Gionn stared at the women washing their clothes on the river bank.

'Arrivèderci,' called Carlo and Enzo as they pulled off the road. 'We are heading for home.' They galloped in the direction of their families' cottages. Carlo turned left and crossed the river to his home, and Enzo turned right, in the direction of the main street and his home above his family's shop. They were bakers originally from Rome.

'We have to continue up the mountains,' Pietro explained. 'Gionn does the town and the surrounding mountains bring back memories?' he asked.

'I'm not too sure. The mountains look familiar, but I don't recognize the town.'

Soon they were in the woods and at the woodcutter's home.

'Papa wrote and told me about a cave, in these woods. The nuns are dragging village folk into the cave and down a passageway that leads into a convent. These people are never seen again. I hate to think what they are doing with them.'

'In your village?' Gionn questioned, very much surprised. 'I can't believe how they get away with it,' Gionn continued.

'I agree with you, but you must realize that the Duke of Savoy owns this land and us. We as a people have no land or country; we are weary pilgrims with only the promise of a better place in heaven. But the butchering must stop, or there will be no Waldensian people left alive. Let's go and see what the woodcutter has to say,' Pietro suggested.

When in the home of the woodcutter Pietro spoke. 'Jacob, I believe they are dragging folk into a cave.'

'Si, terrible it is. Late one night, I woke to the sound of voices. It was a full moon and I was able to see, so I crept outside and stood in the shadows of the trees. There were two carts with people. The children were screaming. They were escaping from Rome and managed to get safely to Pinerolo. While travelling up the mountains they were ambushed by rough-looking soldiers and brought here. Many cloaked people came from somewhere and dragged them into the cave.' He stopped and looked at Pietro who had turned white.

Pietro spoke in a trembling voice. 'We have already been told what happened at Pinerolo to our Barb, Daniel Reveilli. I hate to think what happened to the rest.'

Jacob the woodcutter continued. 'I have been told that many of our people have been hung, quartered, broken upon the wheel, or burned alive at Torino, and their properties confiscated. What hope do we have when they take our properties and place ruffians on them? More spies amongst us, that's what hope they give us,' he sighed.

'Let's go down the cave and see what we can do,' Gionn suggested, flinging off his cape.

Jacob stepped back in shock. Gionn stood there in his Ottoman army uniform. He wore a baggy long-sleeved shirt and baggy pants tucked into knee-high boots. Covering his chest was his breastplate and on his belt in its sheath was a large very sharp sword. He retrieved from his saddlebag a helmet with very long feathers on its side, and he now placed it on his head.

'Good idea, they will be terrified when they see you,' Jacob said.

It was full daylight when Pietro and Gionn entered the cave. Just inside its opening was a room about eight feet square. From this room, there were openings to two underground tunnels. One of these led to the village, into a building used as a convent; the other led to a Catholic church in another part of town.

'Let's try the tunnel on the right,' Pietro suggested.

Soon they saw a light ahead and realized the tunnel led to an outside opening.

'Gionn look at this,' Pietro whispered. 'We are behind a grotto with a statue of Mary standing amongst the flowers.'

'Let's go,' Gionn spoke excitedly.

'Shhhh, a nun is coming this way,' Pietro whispered.

Gionn pushed past Pietro and stood waiting for the nun to kneel in front of Mary, and then he crept up to the statue and stood with his sword drawn in front of him. The nun looked up, unsure of what she was looking at. The setting sun shone on Gionn's breastplate and glistened on his sword. He looked majestic, almost mystical in his bearing. He spoke in his Ottoman tongue. She had never seen or heard anything like it before and fell prostrating herself before him and Mary.

Pietro thought, *'I wonder if she thinks Gionn is an angel.'*

Gionn stepped out of the tunnel and spoke in Patois. 'Take us immediately to the people you dragged from the cart. Do you hear me, Signora? Move now.'

She looked up and Gionn nudged her with his sword. She now stood and practically ran down the path, which led through lawns and lush gardens with high stone walls. She seemed to be heading to the Catholic Church.

'Not so fast Signora,' Gionn hissed, as he quickened his pace. 'Stop now, and change your direction. We will go back through the tunnel and enter through the door into your convent.'

She started to protest.

Gionn gave her a quick poke with his sword, which now tore her tunic and grazed her shoulder. 'Signora back to the grotto and the tunnel. I am aware of the keys hanging from your tunic; I am sure one will be for the convent's door; so, move it, do you hear,' he growled, nudging her on.

After going through the tunnel and the large locked door, she led them into the convent's underground prison and stopped at a barred door, which she unlocked. It was very dark in the cell.

Pietro held the torch in front and called out. 'Paul and Susan Joaquin are you here?'

There was movement from a dark corner and Susan appeared with her three children. She looked dreadful; she was filthy and completely covered in blood. Even her hair was thick and sticky.

'Is Paul here somewhere?' Pietro asked.

She could hardly speak through her swollen lips. 'He's dead.'

'And the others,' he asked, realizing there were only two other people, as well as her and the children, that arrived in the carts.

'They are dead as well,' she managed to murmur.

Gionn this time nudged the nun harder with his sword, while he ripped the keys from her belt. He now pushed the tip of the sword against her tunic and her buttock, and with pleasure felt the tip ripping the cloth and piercing into her flesh. She jumped into the cell screaming in Latin. He left the door ajar so the women could escape. He knew it would take ages before the lock could be changed. Standing there he could hear the prisoners set upon the nun. He also left the door of the tunnel open.

When they came out into the daylight they could see, poor Susan's cuts and bruises. The children followed behind her too scared to cry. Embarrassed and ashamed she held her head down. Without another word, she hobbled quickly in the direction of the woods and home. They looked on saddened by her plight and knew it was better, to just let her go.

They entered Jacob's hut and gave him the keys.

Suddenly a horse galloped up to the woodcutter's door.

An excited voice called to Pietro, 'Pietro, Pietro hurry up you sluggard, I have news for you.'

Pietro recognized Enzo's high-pitched voice and went out to see what all the commotion was about.

'Pietro your folk are in town, at the market. I didn't approach them because I didn't want to spoil your surprise.'

'Now laughing Pietro asked, 'Was Judith with them?'

'I didn't see her, but who knows?'

Before Enzo had finished speaking, Pietro was on his horse. 'Come on Gionn, why so slow?' Laughing they bid Jacob the woodcutter Arrivèderci and galloped to town.

CHAPTER 36

REUNION

Two young signors galloped their horses into Torre
Pellice market piazza. One should have known better.
The people busy with trade looked up and stepped out of
their way. When they saw the Ottoman soldier, fear
overtook them and they rushed from their stalls and
disappeared, leaving all their goods behind. Many tables
were overturned and farm produce was scattered. Pietro's
parents stood staring at the soldier. Suddenly the other
signor jumped from his horse and ran towards them. Their
attention was now drawn to this person in foreign clothes as
he called over and over.

'Papa! Mamma! Papa! Mamma!'

'Papa it's Pietro' cried his mother. She ran past the stalls,
as Pietro ran towards her. Tears filled her eyes, and as they
embraced, she sobbed deeply into his shoulder.

Father also ran, and hugged his son. 'Pietro the soldier
who is he,' whispered father as he looked over Pietro's
shoulder, determined not to take his eyes off the regal figure.

Gionn was now alighting from his horse and
approaching his relatives. Father caught his breath. It was
like his brother was standing in front of him. Mother
thought she was looking at an older version of Marco.

They both spoke together. 'Francesco? Is it Francesco?'

Father shook his head. 'Francesco would be much older
by now.'

It was all too much for Gionn. 'Zia and Zio, I am Gionn,

226

Francesco's son.

They both cried out, and rushed forward, crying and hugging their nephew.

The people crept out and busied themselves picking up their trestles and goods and some just stood there watching and listening to all that was transpiring. Marco appeared from behind their stall and stared at an older version of himself.

Their mother pushed Marco towards his cousin. 'Marco this is Gionn your cugino. His papa, Francesco was your papa's brother. Remember we told you about them.'

Marco nodded.

Pietro looked around. 'Mamma is Judith at the markets.'

'No, it's too dangerous for the children to come to town, so Judith is looking after Maria and baby Ruth at home.'

Pietro swung his leg over his horse. 'Mamma, can you help Gionn? He needs to buy suitable clothes. He has plenty of money and will be able to pay for them, and much more. Is it alright if he comes home with us? I will explain it all when you get home, but I'm off!

'Arrivèderci,' he called, as he galloped from the market piazza, and up the steep hill to home.

PIETRO WITH HIS HEART thumping from excitement ran up the balcony steps. 'Judith, Maria, where are you.' Nobody answered. He went downstairs and out of the courtyard. Standing by the spring-fed faucet he looked up the mountain track, and there they were walking home with the cow slowly trailing behind. He ran towards them. They stopped and watched wondering who he was, and then Judith recognized him. She quickly handed the baby to

Maria and ran with arms outstretched. They fell into each other's arms hugging. 'Pietro, Pietro,' she murmured and looked up at him lovingly.

Maria ran as best as she could, with fat little Ruth on her hips. She handed the baby back to Judith and tried to jump into Pietro's arms. She didn't quite make it, and he had to lift her.

'Pietro, we have been waiting and waiting for you,' she squealed kissing his face all over.

'Young Signorina, I have missed you so much,' he laughed kissing her back. He put Maria down and turned and tried once again to hug Judith but little Ruth stuck out her chubby arms and feet, pushing him away. She turned into her mother's shoulder and cried loudly.

'Maria, could you please take little Ruth back to the house while I speak with Judith,' Pietro requested, and placed the baby into her arms.

'Scusare,' Maria murmured looking cross at him. She trudged with little Ruth on her hip still crying, and she cried too. With her head down she walked into the courtyard without looking back, and the cow followed.

Embracing Judith, he looked down at her. 'Judith, I love you so much. I never want to be away from you again. Will you marry me?'

'Si of course I will. I love you,' and before she finished speaking, he kissed her gently and lovingly on the lips, and she returned his kiss.

WHEN THEY ENTERED THE courtyard, sitting on the steps were two very miserable little girls. Judith took Ruth and rocked her gently in her arms as she fed her. Soon she was fast asleep.

Pietro sat and took his little sister on his knee. 'It's alright Maria, come here and let me give you a big cuddle. You do know I love you, but I had something very special to ask Judith, and when the rest of the family comes home, I will tell all of you, my secret.'

Maria sniffed, wiped her eyes, sat up, and stared at Pietro. 'Tell me, Pietro. Please tell me, and then it can be our secret.' She looked at Judith with pleading eyes.

'Si, tell her Pietro. Maria and I have shared so much while you've been away,' Judith encouraged.

Pietro realized suddenly that Maria would feel betrayed and rejected if he didn't. 'Well, young Signorina you must let me tell the secret to Papa and Mamma when they get back. Now promise and it can be your secret as well.'

'Si si I promise,' squealed Maria now hugging Pietro.

Pietro cleared his throat and looked at Judith with such love, that it made Judith blush. 'Judith and I are getting married, and you can help us. Would you like that?'

'Si, oh how lovely we are getting married,' she squealed, jumping up and hugging Judith.

JUDITH PLACED BABY Ruth in her cradle and gathered chestnuts sitting on the edge of the fire. She placed them in a dish and all three sat around the table breaking off the shells and eating the soft centres. Pietro told happy stories while they waited for the others to return. He dared not tell Judith the terrible truth in front of Maria.

'It's Mamma and Papa, they are home,' Maria squealed, jumping up and rushing to the door. 'Mamma, Papa, I have a surprise for you,' she called over the balcony as her parents opened the courtyard gates.

'She's going to tell,' Pietro hissed.

'Shh, it will be alright. I am sure she won't. Papa has been very firm with her about keeping family secrets and being resilient in difficulties. If she does, she will be in real trouble.'

Maria hung over the balustrade and watched her parents enter the courtyard. After placing the cart and mule in the barn they looked up at her excited little face.

'Mamma I have a surprise for you.'

'Is that so? If it's a secret you had better not tell.'

She jumped up and down as her mother opened the door. 'Surprise Mamma; Pietro is home.' She then ran to Marco, 'Marco, Pietro is home, isn't that so lovely.' She stopped as it wasn't Marco, but somebody that looked like him.

Marco now stepped forward laughing. 'Don't you know what your brother looks like?' he teased.

With the two standing together, she could see there were many differences, but they could certainly pass as brothers.

'Si,' she laughed. 'I wasn't looking properly, was I?'

Everyone laughed and explained to her who Gionn was.

'Now that you are all here,' announced Pietro, 'Judith and I would like to tell you, our secret. I have just proposed to Judith and she has accepted.'

Everyone rushed forward hugging Judith and congratulating Pietro. Amid all the excitement a little voice could be heard. 'Si, we are getting married,' Maria squealed, jumping up and down.

Her father looked very cross. 'Now young Signorina, that's enough, do you hear me?

'Shoosh Papa,' whispered mother, 'little girls think like

that. She knows it's Judith and Pietro that is getting married, but this is her way of being part of it. Si, we Signoras love being part of weddings.' She turned to Maria. 'Come and sit with Judith and me and we will discuss the wedding.' Maria climbed onto her mother's knees. 'You were very good at keeping Judith and Pietro's secret. You are learning, aren't you?'

Maria nodded.

Father went down to the cellar and returned with new wine from his summer harvest.

The men sat around the fire drinking and pulling out chestnuts from the embers and cracking and eating them while discussing past events. The women discussed more pleasant future events.

'Si, I think a wedding before winter would be a good idea,' mother agreed. 'I will tell the others in the village. They too will want to be part of the preparations. Si, we love weddings,' she sighed.

CHAPTER 37

SOLDIERS APPROACHING

*I*n the secluded Angrogna valley with its circle of mountains, the yearly synod was in process. The men and their Barbs discussed the terrible events that had been taking place in their valleys.

Father spoke. 'We are seeing more and more murders and martyr pyres, and for what? We are not thieves, murderers, harlots, or rapists. We are peace-loving and work hard to feed our families, but we pay this high price because we love the Bible. I wish to encourage you to hold fast.'

One of the Barbs stood and spoke. 'Let us ordain our youth here today so we can spread God's word as quickly as we can. They will try and silence us, but God willing we will spread the gospel.'

Many youths stood and stepped forward to a hymn being played.

Mother and Marco left straight after the meeting. They were anxious to get home to Judith, Maria, and baby Ruth who hadn't left the village for over six months as it was far too dangerous. In every sense, to them, the village had become a real ghetto.

Most of the other families at the meeting also left for home, but their men stayed and camped around the fire. They wanted to talk about future precautions needed in their villages. All knew it was only a matter of time before the papal army would be at their doorsteps.

AT DAWN GIONN RODE down the valley through a succession of narrow gorges and then open valleys, walled throughout by the mountains. He was entering Torre Pellice when he saw something. *'Is that a figure, dark against the glare of the early morning sun? Si, it is. It's on the ridge above the gorge, and he's not alone. Oh no! Just look at that; there are hundreds of soldiers. I wonder how many more are hidden behind that ridge,'* he pondered. *'I can't let the soldiers enter into our valleys. I must go back and warn the others.'*

Turning his horse, he galloped back to Pra Del Tor where the meeting had been held.

Gionn thought as he rode into the open valley, *'Si, it's as I thought, the folk are packing their carts for their journey home.'*

They looked up and moved aside as he galloped through their camp and up to the tents of the Barbs. Jumping off his horse before it completely stopped, he held the reins tightly to halt the horse.

'Steady girl, steady now,' he said quietly as he stroked the fidgeting, snorting creature.

The men all ran towards the Barbs' tents. They could see there was something wrong.

Gionn turned to the men and called, 'Soldiers approaching our valley. Many of them! We must be quick so we can ambush them while they're in the narrow gorges. If they approach this valley all will be lost.'

A youth grabbed the horn they used to call the meetings, and soon its sound vibrated through their valley. It was followed by the strident wail of a horn sounding in the distance; others quickly joined it until a shrill, discordant chorus was ringing across the distant hills and valleys, warning others of the impending danger.

MARCO, IN THE HOME pastures, stood listening. *'What was that?'* He thought as he heard the horns echoing across the hills and valleys. Suddenly he recognized the warning and ran down the mountain with the old cow trying to keep up. Mother was standing by the water faucet listening.

'Quickly Marco put the cow away and come with me,' she called. 'We must warn the others in our village.'

Marco knocked on old Antonio's door and nervously looked down the valley while he waited. Soon they opened the door ashen-faced, with their arms filled with blankets and food. 'Mamma said to come to our home as we can lock the courtyard and hide in the cellar.'

'Si we are coming,' replied old Signora Duval.

Marco then ran to their grandfather's house. Grandfather met him on the path with a pike in his hands. 'I'm coming Marco; you go home and I will collect the others,' he offered.

Soon grandfather arrived with his pike in one hand and with his other arm, supporting very old Zio de Vaux; grandfather's brother and the oldest relative of the clan. He lived with his granddaughter Maddy. Her husband Alder Duval was old Antonio's youngest son. She now spoke to the men, as she walked quickly with her newborn in her arms. 'I am so worried about Alder and the signors at the Synod. What will happen to them?' she muttered.

Nobody answered as they didn't want to think of the terrible consequences.

The last little cottage looking up at Mount Baron was visited by mother. 'Hurry along children,' she encouraged. 'We don't know where the soldiers are.'

Her sister Rebecca Duval lived alone with her eighteen-year-old daughter Elizabeth and ten-year-old son Esaye. Her husband, old Antonio's eldest son, a few months earlier died on a martyr pyre at Milano. Now terrified they ran as fast as they could down the narrow village walkway with mother beside them.

When they all arrived, grandfather passed the pike to Marco. 'Antonio and I are going back to his home, as we can see clearly down the valley from there. Lock the gate as soon as I leave. When you hear us blowing the horn take the families down into the cellar. This will be our warning that soldiers are on the pass,' he instructed.

Mother sat the relatives around the fire. 'I will gather blankets when we hear the warning. It will be cold in the cellar, but for now, we may need them up here.'

Old Zio de Vaux sat in the rocking chair next to the fire and fell fast asleep. When the children were fed and settled in the different beds, the women gathered around the table.

'Let's talk about happier things.' Mother suggested noticing fear on her relative's faces. 'Why don't we sort out the arrangements for Judith and Pietro's wedding?'

'I haven't told you,' said her sister Rebecca, trying to lighten the mood. 'Beth has had a regular visitor of late.'

All the women looked up and teased. 'Come on Beth tell us who.'

'Well, Gionn has been courting me,' she said blushing.

'He is a de Vaux which means he isn't blood, so that's good,' smiled her mother.

'Do you think he is serious?' another asked.

Beth blushed and whispered. 'I hope so.'

They now laughed heartily and talked all at once, as was their habit; feeling at peace for the moment, as they shared their bond of kinship.

CHAPTER 38

PAPAL SOLDIERS

ather de Vaux still at the meeting called to the men, 'Go quickly to the homes in this valley and collect all the farm axes, scythes, and knives. Also collect the farm implements that have been fashioned into swords and spears, as crude as they may be. Gather all you can and meet back here. Do it quickly, your families' lives depend on it.'

They did as they were instructed and stood waiting quietly. Their trust in God was renewed and fortified with their time together at the meetings. The fellowship and prayers gave them strength and courage.

Father helped to hand out the implements, but he was furious with the audacity of the soldiers.

THE PAPAL SOLDIERS WITH heads down trudged wearily, two abreast, along the rugged, slippery, narrow tracks, and ahead loomed mountains to ascend, and more gorges to negotiate. The captain hoped when they reached the last valley, they would have time to regroup and have their spears and swords ready to advance and attack.

The soldiers were nearing the end of the gorge when the screeching of birds taking flight filled the air. They stopped and listened to the distant horns. They knew they had been sighted, and the villages were being warned.

IN THE MIDDLE OF THE night light was seen coming up the mountain ridge to the village of Borgata Cyrus. Old Antonio immediately went outside and blew his horn, to warn the others.

Marco, who was sitting at the fire dozing, woke and ran to the others. 'You must wake up. Can't you hear the horn? The soldiers are coming.' His heart raced with fear. 'Wake up; si get your rugs; let's go; quick Mamma.'

He lit a torch and led the way to the cellar. The others followed, dragging blankets and carrying the sleeping children. Marco slammed and locked the cellar door. He stood while everyone settled down in different corners. They were all scared and the older members whispered prayers to the younger ones.

The horn had stopped and Marco knew the soldiers would be very close. 'Perhaps the soldiers have already killed old Antonio and Nonno,' he thought. He now spoke in a quivering voice. 'I'm going to blow out the torch and you mustn't make a sound.' The light went out. Everything was silent, and then a crashing sound at the gates was heard, followed by many footsteps up the stairs and through the house. It seemed only one person came back down. *'I wonder if they know about the cellar,'* Marco thought, sick with fear, and then a voice called at the cellar door.

'Marco it's alright. It's us back from Pra Del Tor.' It was papa. Marco opened the door and everyone rushed out, all talking at once. When they were in the family room what a tale awaited them. The soldiers had turned back, but all knew they would soon return.

What rejoicing and fellowship followed as they prayed with heartfelt thanks for God's protection until the sun rose the next morning.

CHAPTER 39

PROPOSAL

*G*ionn helped Mother Rebecca harvest the last of her corn, and then set to work ploughing her field. Beth walked across the field to him with a jug of water. She laughed at his efforts to hold the reins connected to the plough. Placing her hands over his she explained how it should be done. He looked at her amused. She looked up and blushed deeply dropping her hands.

'Well, I'm a soldier and not a farmer,' Gionn, good-naturedly teased; drinking and wiping his mouth with his sleeve.'

They both spent more time chatting and laughing than working. In the evening he was invited to eat with Beth's family.

While sitting around the family table Mother Rebecca asked; 'Gionn tell us about your life in captivity.'

Gionn laughed. He knew he could tell them many terrible tales but he chose instead to relate the happy times. 'Well, I was captured and sold to the Ottoman army as a slave at ten years of age. I was placed in the Kapikuku unit. Our job as small boys was to serve the Sultan and I worked very hard and did all I was told.' He especially said all of this for the benefit of ten-year-old Esaye who was listening intently. 'When I was fifteen years old, I was placed in the Janissary unit and became one of the Sultan's bodyguards. We were all paid a wage. Eventually, I was placed in charge of his troops. I had a very important role to play and was treated more like a trusted family member than a slave. The sultan, Prince Mehmed, treated me like a son.' He stopped and looked at their faces. 'Never mind about all of that, I have chosen to be here with you, and I want to learn your ways, and become part of your household.

Mother Rebecca caught her breath and swung around to look at her daughter, who sat mesmerized with Gionn. 'Please scusare, I have jobs to do. Come on Esaye come and help Mamma,' and together they left the room.

Gionn stood to leave. 'Well sweet Signorina,' he said while standing at the door, 'It's time for me to leave.'

Beth stood close, looking up into his eyes. He impulsively drew her into his arms and kissed her. She drew back shocked. He saw her embarrassment and left.

Gionn arrived very early the next morning. The sun had hardly risen. 'Today I have to hurry with the chores as I have some business to attend to in Torre Pellice,' he explained.

Beth was concerned about Gionn's beliefs, and as they worked together in the garden, she stole secret looks at him. 'Does *he know and understand our beliefs, especially,*' she thought, '*after last night, how many signorinas' has he kissed.*' The thought made her very jealous.

She spoke shyly, 'Gionn, I was wondering, do you understand our beliefs?' She now blushed, as she thought of his kiss.

'Sort of,' he answered. 'I never forgot my family's teachings and always carried around text from the Bible.' He pulled out scraps of paper from his pockets, with his name written on the top of the pages. 'I have tried to remember how to read the writing and tried not to forget my native tongue. I believe in God and the Commandments. The

Commandments have been impossible to keep as a soldier, but I haven't taken other signorinas' if that's what you are worried about?'

She went very red and dropped her head.

'*Ah, that's the problem,*' He thought. '*I must be more careful as she might turn me down.*'

'Beth?'

She looked up, and he watched her closely, he spoke in their tongue with his Turkish accent. 'I have been away most of my life and I need you to teach me your ways.'

She nodded, looking at him shyly.

He thought, '*What a beautiful young signorina. She is so kind and gentle. I must make her mine as quickly as I can.*'

GIONN GALLOPED HIS HORSE down the narrow pass to Torre Pellice. He wanted to visit the woodcutter and he also had other business in the town to attend to. He especially wanted to get back to Beth.

He met the woodcutter on the edge of the woods clearing broken branches. 'Buongiorno,' Gionn greeted and alighted from his horse. 'Did you go down the tunnel and try out the keys?' He asked.

'Si, I did and the doors were still open. They were just as you left them. I went down to the cells and they were all empty. I then walked through the building and there wasn't a person to be seen. I think they took off in fear of being attacked by a strange army. An Ottoman army, if I am not mistaken,' he laughed.

'Praise the Lord,' Gionn replied as he climbed back on his horse. 'Don't forget to keep watch. You never know when they will decide once again to start their nonsense.

'Arrivèderci,' he called.

'Arrivèderci,' responded the woodcutter and he waved.

GIONN WENT TO THE silversmith's shop. When the shopkeeper saw him, he reached up to a shelf and brought down two small highly polished steel trays. On each tray were two steel long-stemmed goblets, with a pattern of grapes around the rim. On the side was carved a shield with a name in its centre. The names on each goblet were Judith and Pietro, and on the other tray, the goblets had Beth and Gionn. There was one cup for each of them.

When Gionn paid the money, the shopkeeper explained, 'Your breastplate and helmet certainly had more metal than we thought. We had quite a bit left over which has made the cost of crafting these goblets and trays much cheaper than I first thought.'

'Grazie, they are wonderful. Just the thing for the brides and grooms,' Gionn said grinning.

That evening he was excited as he walked over to Beth's. His chance to talk to her alone came when Mother Rebecca left the room to settle Esaye in bed.

'Beth, I have something to show you.'

Beth looked at his flushed excited face and held her breath.

He stepped outside and brought in a box, and carefully removed the contents wrapped in old soft cloths. He placed down a tray and arranged two goblets with the name of Pietro and Judith. They shone and glittered in the lamps flickering candlelight. 'This is their wedding present. Do you think they will like it?

'Oh Si,' she whispered. 'They are beautiful.'

He then placed down the other tray and arranged two goblets on it, with the name of Gionn on one and Beth on the other. These are wedding presents as well. Beth, I love you, and I want to marry you.'

She sucked in her breath and stood there silent, staring at him.

'I know it's only been a few short weeks, but it feels so right and I can't stand being away from you, not even for a moment. What do you say? Will you marry me sweet, shy Beth?' He asked pleadingly, gathering her in his arms.

Once in his arms, she felt safe and protected. She looked up into his caring face and knew it felt right. 'Si of course I will,' she answered somewhat choked. He now kissed her lovingly and she returned his kiss.

'Mamma, come and see what Gionn has bought. Gionn has something to ask you, Mamma.'

Her mother already knew as Gionn had asked her permission weeks earlier before he started courting Beth, and of course, she had given her consent.

THE ABLE-BODIED MEN in the village gathered their last season's crops and vegetables and headed in their carts to the market in Torre Pellice. Ten-year-old Esaye tagged along, under the watchful eye of Marco.

All the women, baby, and old Zio de Vaux went to Mamma de Vaux's cottage. 'Today,' announced mother, 'We are going to sort out wedding plans for the two couples.'

All were very excited, as they had never before had a double wedding in their small village.

'Where will Pietro and Judith live?' One of the women asked.

'Mamma has kindly given us the downstairs rooms,' Judith answered. 'There is a fireplace in the middle of the two rooms. We will use one as a bedroom and the other as our family room. I will be able to cook most of our meals down there and when I need to bake bread, I will use Mamma's oven up here.'

'Si,' continued mother with laughter as she waved her hands in the direction of the courtyard, 'Marco will have to use the room across the courtyard. There isn't a fireplace over in those rooms, so I don't know how he will fare in winter.'

'Don't worry,' butted in old Signora Duval. 'I have a spare fur blanket, he can have. You can sleep right out in the snow and be warm under a fur.'

'What about Beth and Gionn?' Another asked.

Rebecca answered, 'They will be fine. They will have Beth's room.' They all laughed.

The women brought out dresses that they had worn on their wedding day, and Judith and Beth tried them on. When a suitable dress was chosen, they stood on the table while the women pinned, cut, and fastened extra bits until the garments fitted and looked perfect. Later they would carefully stitch the alterations.

Everyone wanted to be part of all the wedding plans, so now they turned their attention to sorting out the wedding menu and preparations.

Early in the evening, the men returned from the market. They too had a surprise for Judith and Beth.

'Well, open the parcels and see if you like what Gionn and I have bought you,' Pietro urged. In the parcels were two exquisite, finely woven, white lace shawls, and lace bonnets to match. Each shawl was slightly different. 'They are to be worn with the wedding dresses,' Pietro explained.

'Well, are they suitable for the big day,' Gionn urged as he watched them examine and pass the shawls and bonnets around the table to the other women, who admired the fine lace; all talking at once.

'Well, what do you think,' Gionn grinning asked once again, as Father de Vaux stood there with his hands on his hips.

The women stopped talking and looked up. 'Si, si,' chorused many excited voices.

Maria jumped up and down clapping her hands and yelling louder than everyone. 'Si, si they are just so, so, beautiful.'

Esaye standing next to her, gave her a poke, as her father was watching, but he just shook his head at Maria and laughed, and the other men in the village also laughed; well amused with all the excitement in the room.

Judith spoke, 'The presents are lovely. Can we afford them?'

The bridegrooms nodded laughing, and Beth stood there speechless, smiling up at Gionn.

CHAPTER 40

DOUBLE WEDDING

Pietro took his mother aside. 'Mamma, while we were away, Gionn and I saved some money and we are going to help you with the reception. We've made arrangements in Torre Pellice to have sweet pastries, and cakes made by Enzo's Mamma in their bakery. We also ordered two traditional Angrogna wedding cakes, with lots of dried fruit and nuts. Tell the Signoras about it, but please don't tell our brides. We want to give them a surprise.'

'Si Grazie, Grazie, it will be a great help for everyone, as we have only one week to organize and cook everything,' mother explained kissing Pietro.

THE WOMEN INDUSTRIOUSLY fixed bridal dresses, made bread, killed hens, and plucked and stuffed them. Mother used her cow's fresh milk to prepare bocconcini cheese. She also made fresh butter, and two days before the wedding she put aside fresh cream for fruit that was stored in the cellar. The men in the village brought their best wine and juice and placed them in the cellar for the big day.

'Marco, could you come up the mountain with me, to collect rocks?' His father called. 'The days are becoming cold. I thought we could build a fireplace in our courtyard. I believe this is where the Signorinas want the service to be held.'

This is the ancient villa in the story. The courtyard where the wedding was held. The balcony where they enter the top rooms. The lower where the cow is kept. It is over 500 years old.

'I think we should build them today, as its Thursday and the weddings are Sunday morning,' father suggested.

Soon there was a large fireplace. Later Marco swept the cobbled courtyard and the other men placed sticks and logs on the hearth.

Nonno called out, 'Will we be sitting or standing for the service.'

Pietro answered, 'Our Signorinas said to stand. It will be better that way as we have asked our entire village and many from Torre Pellice.'

Mother had just finished milking the cow, stepped out of the barn, and sighed as she thought to herself, *'I don't know where we will put them all.'*

When she entered the family room, she looked around and realized they wouldn't have enough chairs and the table was far too small. She voiced her concerns to Pietro.

'Don't worry Mamma, we will shift all the furniture out of this room first thing Sunday morning, and bring in tables and chairs from the other cottages. We should have four large tables and who would know how many chairs.'

Very early Sunday morning, a large tub with hot water was placed in Mother de Vaux's bedroom and the brides were first to bathe. When they finished, they sat in the parlour by the fireside, drying and braiding their hair, while the rest of the family took their turn to bathe.

Marco swept the long parlour's wooden floor and Pietro and Gionn and the other men of the village carried across the tables and chairs. They then went outside and lit the fires.

'Well look who's early,' Gionn laughed as he carried chairs into the courtyard.

Carlo and Enzo tied their mule to the rail and started emptying their cart. 'We have four large baskets of goodies for you. Where do you want them?' Enzo asked swinging his arm in the direction of the stairs and nearly spilling the basket's contents.

'Si Grazie, just take them upstairs. The Signorinas will be thrilled when they see our surprise.' Gionn replied, and went over and peeked into the baskets. 'Si they are just the thing. I'm hungry already,' he laughed.

The girls looked up from the hearth and stared in amazement at Enzo and Carlo as they carefully placed the cakes and pastries on the back tables. When they came back the second time, they each gingerly carried a wedding cake which they placed in the middle of each table.

'Look what Gionn and Pietro have organized for us,' squealed Beth, as she hugged Judith.

Maria in her new dress, brought home by Pietro, carried little Ruth on her hip. They both had to stay clean. She walked outside the courtyard and looked down the narrow lane. 'Mamma, Papa, I can hear them coming,' she excitedly called.

Many voices in song, carried up the valley. Soon they turned a corner and she could see them. There were people on horses, families in carts pulled by mules, and others walking. All were bringing presents and food.

Maria ran back to the courtyard gates as best as she could with baby Ruth in her arms. 'Everybody, they are here. The guests are here,' She shouted at the top of her lungs.

Baby Ruth's lip dropped and she bellowed even louder. Pietro who was walking up to them, leaned over and lifted the baby onto his hip, and then shook the Barb's hand, as he alighted from his horse.

The arriving guests gathered around the lit fires and warmed their hands. The morning was brisk and cold with the towering mountains covered in mist.

Mother was dressed and now helped the brides to dress

and prepare.

Deep male voices could be heard and the women inside stopped and listened. The men sang a well-known hymn, and they all knew it was time to go down to the courtyard. The women bowed their heads in prayer and then Judith and Beth side by side walked down the stairs. Gionn turned around and winked at Beth and she nearly lost her footing. Blushing she held the rail and walked beside Judith. They took their places next to Pietro and Gionn.

Mother and the other village women watched from the balcony. She caught her breath, as it reminded her of their wedding day. Wiping the tears from her eyes she whispered to Maria, who handed baby Ruth to her. 'Stay here with us dear. You can see better up here. Oh, isn't it so lovely?'

As the visiting Barb conducted the service the opened courtyard doors seem to form a frame around them, with the green fields and towering mountains as nature's beautiful backdrop. The sun broke through the mist, bathing them and making the framed picture glow.

Each couple said their wedding vows as they looked lovingly at their partners, and when the ceremony was finished, the people watching the scene joined together in a joyful song. Soon all went upstairs to the wedding feast.

The long family room looked wonderful with two tables down the middle, and two tables against the back wall that held the cakes. To add to all of this the visitors brought in their gifts, and their food was now placed on the tables.

The guests settled in chairs at the tables and each bride opened their lovely homemade gifts and passed them around for all to admire. While they were thus entertained the men opened the drinks, and the village women returned from their cottages with roast chicken, and vegetables, which they placed on the already food-laden tables, and mother removed hot pizzas from her oven.

What merriment and comradeship followed, as they laughed and toasted the two young couples with lots of speeches and stories, some sad but most amusing.

Beth lovingly looked at Gionn as he told his stories. He looked down at her turned-up face and tapped her nose and whispered in his thick Turkish accent. 'Well, that is how it was, my sweet Signorina.' Everybody heard and laughed.

Eventually, Judith went to Mother de Vaux's room to nurse baby Ruth. When the child was asleep, she placed her in the cradle and returned to Pietro. She leaned over and spoke softly to him, and he reached up and kissed her cheek.

The fire crackled and burned with a glow of colour, giving warmth to the cold day. They sang all their favourite hymns, and eventually cleared a spot on the table to study the Bible, which was something they loved to do.

The evening was approaching, and the narrow pass to Torre Pellice would soon be dark. The guest stepped outside and pulled their hoods well over their heads. A cold wind blew up the valley. The men lit their torches, and sang their songs, as they carefully negotiated the slippery mountain track, back to their homes.

CHAPTER 41

WAR

A shepherd's hut

*E*arly next morning horns in the distance could be heard echoing through the mist-covered valleys. Father lay in his bed listening. '*Where are they coming from?*' he wondered, and as he listened, he realized the horns were sounding in Torre Pellice. 'It didn't take Cataneo, long to gather reinforcements,' he thought fearfully. 'I must warn the others.'

Many horns, in a discordant chorus, echoed from village to village in the Angrogna valley. The people hurriedly gathered their families and made arrangements to move to

Pra Del Tor.

Soon folk were passing the village, Borgata Cyrus. On their backs, they carried their kneading troughs, their ovens, and other culinary utensils. Some carried their aged on their shoulders, and their sick on couches. The small children held their parents' hands as they began to climb the hills in the direction of the Pra Del Tor. It was safer and easier to leave their horses and carts behind. Transporting their household things, they could be seen crossing the rugged paths.

Mother quickly gathered what she could of the wedding banquet, plus blankets and clothes, placing them in packs. Old Zio de Vaux was placed on a couch that was to be carried by Marco and Nonno. Baby Ruth was placed in a sling in front of Judith and a pack was tied to Judith's back. All were laden down with household things.

The men busied themselves collecting their manufactured pikes and other weapons of defence and attack. They carried these weapons with their bows and wore their skin-covered bucklers made with bark, to resist any offending pikes. They all now pressed forward with their families to the Pra Del Tor, where they would be in a better situation to resist the oncoming attacks.

When they reached their destination for that day, the men set about repairing the old barricades and arranging themselves into fighting parties. They assigned to the various corps the posts they were to defend. In the hollow behind, protected by the rising ground on which fathers, husbands, and brothers were posted, were numbers of women and children, gathered there for shelter.

Mother spoke to Maria, 'I want you to sit with Judith and

baby Ruth under the bushes' low-hanging branches, and play a game of hiding and seek. If strange soldiers appear you must stay in hiding. Just do as Judith tells you.'

The papal army was close behind those fleeing. They realized their foe would be hiding behind mountain ridges or in the thickets, so they discharged a shower of arrows as they advanced, and the Waldensian line on which these missiles fell, seemed to waver, and be on the point of giving away, as many men were killed or wounded.

Pietro quickly went from one group to another, to check for the living.

Mother de Vaux and the others with her, behind the line, realized the danger. They fell on their knees, extending their hands in supplication to God. They cried, 'O God of our fathers, help us! O God, deliver us!' The children hid and were silent.

That cry was heard by the attacking host, and especially by one of its captains; the Black Mondovi, a proud, bigoted, bloodthirsty man.

'My soldiers will answer,' he shouted with horrible blasphemies, raising his visor as he spoke. At that instant an arrow from the bow of Pierre Revel, of Angrogna, entered between his eyes, piercing through his skull, and he fell on the earth a corpse. The fall of this daring leader disheartened the papal army. The soldiers began to fall back. They were chased down the slopes by the Vaudois, who now descended upon them like one of their mountain torrents. Having driven their invaders down to the plain, and cutting off and killing many in their flight, they returned as the evening began to fall, to celebrate with songs, on the heights where they had won the victory.

The children enjoyed a feast of left-over wedding food, and listened to the stories of victory, as they all sat around the campfires.

In the morning Pietro spoke to his mother. 'Mamma I know how to get the family into another valley, and away from the fighting.'

'Si, let's do that,' she answered gathering her things and their family members.

Soon they were on their way. After many hours Pietro left the women and children, plus the elderly, in a deserted shepherd's hut that still had a small amount of food and wood in its cellar. Marco stayed with them as he could hunt and knew his way around the mountains and valleys.

CATANEO BURNED WITH rage and shame at being defeated by these simple herdsmen. While he was reassembling his army the Waldenses escaped along the chasm that entered Angrogna.

He led his soldiers now into the narrow defiles. Here great rocks overhung the path. Also, mighty chestnut trees flung their branches across the way, veiling it in gloom, and far down below thundered the mountain torrent that watered the valley. Still advancing he found himself without fighting, in a wide-open valley. He was now the master of the Val di Angrogna.

He and his army passed numerous cottages with their finely cultivated fields and vineyards, on the left of the torrent. But he could see none of the inhabitants. These he knew were in the hidden valley of the Pra de Tor. Between him and his prey rose the 'Barricade' a steep un-scalable mountain, forming a wall across the valley.

Cataneo spoke to his captain. 'Surely, we didn't come all this way to end our march here. These people have a way through, but where?'

Cataneo was in a vast cul-de-sac. He could see the white peaks around the Pra, but between him and the Pra itself was the Barricade blocking his way. He searched and, unhappily for him, he found the entrance. Some convulsion of nature had rent the mountains, and through the long, narrow, dark chasm lay the only path that led to the head of Angrogna.

Cataneo called to his men. 'We have found the pass. They are hiding on the other side. Today we will complete our duties and rid ourselves of these people. Let us march into this gorge to the other side, and finish our work.'

The only pathway through the chasm was a rocky ledge on the side of the mountain, so narrow that not more than two abreast could advance along it. If assailed either in front or in the rear, or from above, there was absolutely no retreat. The pathway hung midway between the bottom of the gorge and the summit of the mountain. Here the naked cliff ran sheer up for at least one thousand feet. When they came through, there was a half-acre or so of level space giving standing room on the mountain's side. The soldiers would now have to negotiate the second terrifying chasm, which ran on for another one or two miles. Towards the end of the gorge, it opened into an Amphitheatre of meadows of dimensions so goodly, that an entire nation could find room to encamp in it. This is where the Angrogna Waldenses now took refuge.

So, into this terrible chasm, the soldiers of the papal legate now marched. They kept advancing, as best they could, along the narrow ledge. Assembled in the meadow like an Amphitheatre, the Waldensian people had but one entrance to guard, and the Papal soldiers, so Cataneo believed, were to sever that position in one blow. But God was watching over the Waldenses.

JUDITH SPOKE TO THE children huddled together in the shepherd's hut, which was high on the mountain looking down over the gorge. 'God has said to the papal soldiers. I will put my hook in thy nose, and my bridle in thy lips, and I will cause thee to return by the way which thou came.'

'How will God do that, Judith?' Maria laughed at the thought.

'Maybe almighty angels will block the pass,' Judith continued.

'Si, si, that's it,' Maria answered.

'Or maybe it will be with thunderbolts and hailstorms,' Judith continued.

'Si that's it,' Maria laughed clapping her hands.

It wasn't any of these, but God hadn't forgotten His faithful true people. The instrumentality now put in motion to shield the Waldenses from destruction, was one of the lightest and frailest of all nature.

'Look, Maria, look what God has sent to save our people?' Judith said as she pointed to something down the valley.

Keenly watched by Judith and her family and the Vaudois soldiers, was a white cloud no bigger than a man's hand. It gathered on the mountain's summit, and at about the same time, the army was entering the chasm. Unobserved by the papal soldiers, it grew rapidly bigger and blacker and began to descend. It came rolling down the mountain's side, wave after wave like an ocean tumbling out of heaven, falling into the chasm in which the Papal army was passing through; sealing it up and filling it from top to bottom with thick black fog. In a moment the soldiers were in the night; they were bewildered, stupefied, and could see neither ahead nor behind. They couldn't advance or retreat. They halted in a state of terror.

A cheer went up by the Vaudois in the valley. 'Look what God has done for us,' Gionn called. 'Let's get the invaders.'

Climbing the slopes of the Pra, and issuing from all their hiding places, they spread themselves over the mountain's paths, which were familiar to them. The soldiers stood riveted beneath them, caught in the double toils of the chasm and the mist. The Waldenses tore up huge stones and rocks and sent them thundering down into the ravine. The Papal soldiers were crushed where they stood. Nor was this all, Gionn and some of the Waldenses boldly entered the chasm, with a sword in hand, and attacked them in front.

Consternation seized the papal soldiers. Panic impelled them to flee, but their effort to escape was more fatal than the sword of the Waldenses. They jostled one another and threw each other down in the struggle. Some were trodden to death. Others were rolled over the precipice, and crushed on the rocks below, or drowned in the torrent, and so perished miserably.

Captain Saquet a gigantic man like his Philistine prototype vented terrible curses to the Waldensian dogs. The words were yet in his mouth when his foot slipped. He rolled over the precipice, tumbled into the torrent of Angrogna, and was carried away by the stream. His body was finally deposited in a deep eddy or whirlpool, called in the country a 'tompie' from the noise made by its waters.

THE WAR HUNG ABOVE the valleys, like a cloud for a whole year. It inflicted much suffering and loss upon the Waldenses; their homes were burned, their fields destroyed, their goods carried off, and their people slain.

A THIN, WORN, RAGGED family came from a shepherd's hut, high on the mountain slope. They marched home to their village Borgata Cyrus, sweetly singing hymns, as they negotiated the decline. They had lost old Zion de Vaux who died in his sleep, and Maddy's infant, because the conditions were severe. Also in earlier skirmishes, they lost their Nonno, and old Antonio Duval. From Torre Pellice they lost their beloved, happy friend, Enzo. But the miracles that God had performed in the Pra Del Tor would never be forgotten.

THE INVADERS SUFFERED heavier losses than they inflicted. Of the 18,000 regular troops, to which we may add about an equal number of desperadoes, with which the campaign opened, few ever returned to their homes. They left their bones on the mountains they had come to subdue.

EPILOGUE

Faced with the spread of the Reformation throughout Europe, the Church of Rome assembled the 'Council of Trent,' which imposed a new discipline on religious life that was destined to last for centuries. The contrast between these two groups led to brutal religious wars throughout the continent.

Cardinals and Catholic theologians formed the assembly that made up the court of the 'Inquisition,' and they developed the Index of Prohibited Books. They attempted to stifle freedom of conscience. With the renewal of this religious order came a vast campaign of propaganda, intending to establish Catholicism everywhere.

Having adhered to the Reformation meant that the Waldenses were at the mercy of Catholic armies with diverse results depending on the area in which they lived.

The Luberon colonies (south of France) were destroyed in 1545.

The Waldenses in Cabrio were exterminated in June 1561.

In the Duchy of Savoy, on the other hand, the Waldenses of the valleys managed to resist the attacks of Emanuele Filiberto's troops, and in the same year, they signed an agreement that gave them the right to practice their religion, on the condition they did not convert others.

In the valleys of Piedmont in the 17th century brief periods of peace alternated with periods of brutal repression by the Duke of Savoy and the Popes' Inquisition. The echo of the massacre of 1655 provoked indignation throughout

Europe.

For 150 years the Waldenses lived isolated in their valleys as if they were in a real ghetto.

In 1730 all the edicts concerning the Waldenses were collected together in a legal document which led to the Waldenses being hemmed in by legal restrictions. This however did not prevent contacts which helped them survive.

Only the French Revolution and Napoleon brought a ray of hope to this marginalized, the cultured little world. But from the fall of Napoleon until 1848, there was a return to the restoration of the Catholic monarchy and Catholicism.

HISTORIC FACTS AND DATES

Waldenses

Year 364: Vigilantius preaching in the
Cottian Alps.

600: Columbanus taught the original pure
faith and ran training colleges in Bobbio
Italy.

800: Waldensian forebears in the Valley
of Piedmont.

817: Claude Bishop of Torino taught
Justification by faith alone.

1173: Peter Waldo founder of 'Poor men
of Lyon'.

1315: Waldensian settlement in southern
Italy; established and prospered.

Period of story

1486: Papal Bull calling for the
extirpation of the heretics.

1487 Archdeacon of Cremona appointed
Legate of Pope Innocent VIII

1488:3000 Suffocated in a cave
Cataneo attacks –hundreds of soldiers
drown in the torrent of Angrogna.

Correct historic dates in the novel

1432–1492 Pope Innocent VIII
1452–1519 Leonardo da Vinci

Character placed in a slightly different time in novel correct dates below

1500–1571 Benevento the goldsmith

Placed in a slightly different time in the novel

1453–1478 Ottoman army-controlled Venezia
1478 Conspiracy to kill Lorenzo and his brother Giuliano
1478 Lorenzo adopted his illegitimate son.
1495–1498 Leonardo was commissioned to paint 'Last Supper' in Dominican Church in Milano took three years to complete work.

ITALIAN VERNACULAR

Si	yes
Signora	women
Signor	man
Signorina	unmarried woman
Mamma	mother
Papa	father
Nonno	grandfather
Cugino	cousin
Bambino	baby boy
Bambina	baby girl
Amico's	friends
Stupido	stupid
Arrivèderci	goodbye
Buongiorno	good morning
Patois	Waldensian dialect

www.ingramcontent.com/pod-product-compliance
Lightning Source LLC
Chambersburg PA
CBHW060908120626
46553CB00001B/243